DATE DUE			
20			
20			
20			

CHATHAM HOUSE PAPERS · 38

THE SOVIET UNION AND CUBA

CHATHAM HOUSE PAPERS

General Series Editor: William Wallace
Soviet Foreign Policy Programme Director: Alex Pravda

Chatham House Papers are short monographs on current policy problems which have been commissioned by the Royal Institute of International Affairs. In preparing the paper, authors are advised by a study group of experts convened by the RIIA. Publication of the paper by the Institute indicates its standing as an authoritative contribution to the public debate.

The Royal Institute of International Affairs is an independent body which promotes the rigorous study of international questions and does not express opinions of its own. The opinions expressed in this publication are the responsibility of the author.

CHATHAM HOUSE PAPERS · 38

THE SOVIET UNION AND CUBA

Peter Shearman

The Royal Institute of International Affairs

Routledge & Kegan Paul
London, New York and Andover

First published 1987
by Routledge & Kegan Paul Ltd
11 New Fetter Lane, London EC4P 4EE
29 West 35th Street, New York, NY 10001, USA, and
North Way, Andover, Hants SP10 5BE

Reproduced from copy supplied by
Stephen Austin and Sons Ltd and
printed in Great Britain by
Redwood Burn Limited
Trowbridge, Wiltshire

Library of Congress Cataloging-in-Publication Data

Shearman, Peter, 1950-
The Soviet Union and Cuba.

(Chatham House papers ; 38)
1. Soviet Union – Foreign relations – Cuba.
2. Cuba – Foreign relations – Soviet Union.
3. Cuba – Foreign relations – 1959-   .
4. Soviet Union – Foreign relations– 1945-
I. Title.   II. Series: Chatham House papers ; no. 38.
DK69.3.C9S54   1987   327.4707291   87-4689

ISBN 0-7102-1229-1

CONTENTS

ABBREVIATIONS

CIA	Central Intelligence Agency
CMEA	Council for Mutual Economic Assistance
CPSU	Communist Party of the Soviet Union
EC	European Community
EPLF	Eritrean People's Liberation Front
FLN	Front de la Libération Nationale
FNLA	National Front for the Liberation of Angola
FSLN	Sandinista Front for National Liberation
MPLA	Popular Movement for the Liberation of Angola
NAM	Non-Aligned Movement
NEP	New Economic Policy
NIEO	New International Economic Order
NJM	New Jewel Movement
OAU	Organization of African Unity
PCC	Communist Party of Cuba
PMAC	Provisional Military Council
PRA	People's Revolutionary Army
PRC	People's Republic of China
PRG	People's Revolutionary Government
PSP	Popular Socialist Party
UNITA	National Union for the Total Independence of Angola

ACKNOWLEDGMENTS

I would like to thank three scholars who provided useful comments on an earlier draft of this paper: Roy Laird, Mike Bowker and Alex Pravda. In addition, the participants of a Chatham House study group helped to clarify many issues for me. Nigel Pearce of Chatham House was of great assistance in preparing the manuscript for publication. Finally, I gratefully acknowledge the financial support of the ESRC (grant no. E00222011).

August 1987   P.S.

1
INTRODUCTION

Given the importance of the Soviet-Cuban connection in global politics, it is remarkable that West Europeans have not sought to gain a full understanding of a relationship which is often at the centre of US concerns. The Soviet-Cuban connection has bedevilled successive American presidents and has contributed to or caused a number of US/Soviet crises, from the missile crisis of 1962, through the Cienfuegos submarine issue in 1970, to the 'mini' crisis of the Soviet combat brigade in 1979. Furthermore, the decisive role of the Soviet Union and Cuba in regional conflicts in Africa in the 1970s (most notably in Angola and the Horn) was instrumental in undermining superpower detente. The US-led invasion of Grenada in October 1983, in the words of President Reagan, saved the small Caribbean island from becoming a 'victim' of 'Cuban and Soviet internationalism'. Central America has been in crisis for some seven years, and during this period it has come to be the most troublesome and divisive issue in US foreign policy since the Vietnam war. Again, the Soviet-Cuban connection is considered by many in the United States to be a key factor: in a glossy, colourful handbook, replete with photographs of Cuban children armed with Soviet weapons, maps of the Caribbean with threatening arrows signifying Soviet ships blocking sea-lanes, and tables showing Soviet arms transfers, the US Departments of State and Defense make it clear how they view Soviet intentions. The USSR is seen as the principal instigator of unrest in the region, whose purpose, through its Cuban 'proxy', is to spread 'communist subversion' throughout the Caribbean.[1]

1

Introduction

This paper examines the underlying patterns of the Cuban-Soviet relationship as it has developed since the revolution that overthrew General Fulgencio Batista in 1959; it seeks to uncover who influences whom, where, when, why and how, and assesses the changes that have taken place over time. In particular it examines the thesis that Cuba acts as a satellite, surrogate, or proxy for Moscow in conducting its policies in Africa and Central America.

The paper begins by tracing the development of Soviet-Cuban ties following the Cuban revolution of 1959. This development can be seen in three stages, starting with the initial Soviet reaction to the revolution and Khrushchev's opportunistic strategy of gaining influence in the Third World through large injections of economic and military aid. After Khrushchev's ouster in 1964, the collective leadership under Brezhnev embarked upon a more pragmatic policy towards the Third World, and during this second period – from the mid-1960s to the early 1970s – tensions existed between Moscow and Havana over the appropriate means for achieving socialist revolution in the Third World. The third period saw Cuba integrated into the socialist bloc's economic system, the first such state outside Moscow's direct sphere of influence to gain admittance to the Council for Mutual Economic Assistance (CMEA). It is this period that is of most interest, for it was in the 1970s and 1980s, when Cuba was totally dependent upon the USSR for its economic survival and national security, that the Soviet-Cuban link became so important in regional conflicts. The core of the paper therefore takes the form of case studies of Soviet and Cuban behaviour in four conflict situations: the Angolan civil war, the war between Ethiopia and Somalia, the Grenadian revolution and the Nicaraguan revolution. The final chapter sets out the conclusions arising from the case studies and the implications these have for devising an appropriate British and West European policy towards the Soviet Union and Cuba.

One basic aim of the paper is to assess the extent to which the Soviet Union influences the conduct of Cuban foreign policy. It will therefore be useful at this stage to refer briefly to the question of measuring 'influence' in a bilateral relationship. It is extremely difficult to identify empirically where influence has been used and how far it has proved effective. It is not sufficient simply to measure quantifiable objective power attributes (e.g., economic or military strength, technological development and natural resources) and deduce that an asymmetry in any of these capabilities, in which one state is heavily dependent upon the other, translates into influence. That economic dependence does not neatly translate into political influence for the benefactor in a patron/client relationship is evidenced by the lack of leverage the United States had over Israeli actions in the Lebanon in 1982. Similarly in the 1960s, when Cuba was already heavily economically dependent upon the Soviet Union, Fidel Castro's policies in Latin America ran directly counter to Soviet interests. Another example is Egypt in the 1970s, when Sadat, despite being heavily dependent on the Soviet Union for military supplies, engaged in activities opposed in Moscow. Dependency on one side does not automatically mean an equivalent degree of influence for the other.

It is of course a contested proposition that influence can only be identified in observable behaviour,[2] but for the purposes of this paper I shall assume that an examination of Cuban and Soviet activity in Africa and Central America during the past ten years, and of Cuban and Soviet interactions in these regions, will reveal who influenced whom. Exercising influence, like exercising other forms of power, usually implies one actor, A, getting another actor, B, to do something it would not otherwise do.[3] In order to gain influence state A can generally employ either carrots or sticks, promises or threats, to gain B's compliance with an action that it, state B, would otherwise not have taken. This can involve the direct use of force, economic sanctions, the threat of punishment, the granting of economic rewards, the offer of rewards, or persuasion.

In the case studies which follow the historical background, these instruments for gaining influence will be considered in order to determine whether influence has indeed been used. The fundamental difficulty here relates to the very nature of a Marxist-Leninist political system. In an 'influence relationship' *communication* is essential, since state A needs to convey to state B that if a certain act is or is not carried out, then certain rewards or punishments will be awarded or denied. Communication within and between Soviet-type political systems, to the great frustration of Western politicians and scholars, is conducted in such secrecy that it is usually impossible to be absolutely certain that we understand the motivations and goals of their policies and actions. For example, it is no secret what motivated the US economic embargo against Cuba, and what the objective of such a policy was. The documentary evidence is readily available in Congressional hearings, newspaper reports, interviews and memoir literature. With regard to the USSR and Cuba, however, there is no such readily available documentation on the Soviet decision to reduce the increase in oil supplies to Cuba and to delay the signing of an economic agreement in 1968, although this is generally seen in the West as an example of the Kremlin putting pressure on Cuba to modify its international behaviour.

We are left with no alternative, when dealing with such secretive societies, but to use our own judgment when comparing the little information we have with the behaviour that we observe. We have also to be very careful in analysing Soviet and Cuban literature, but, as Jerry Hough displays convincingly in a recent study of Soviet scholarly writings, it is nevertheless possible to identify from them changing Soviet perceptions and policy priorities.[4] This is an important point, since the case studies in this paper of the Soviet-Cuban link in regional conflicts are based in large part on relevant Soviet Russian-language and Cuban Spanish-language sources as well as on research trips to both Moscow and Havana.

2
THE EARLY YEARS

Soviet Third World policy and the Cuban revolution
By the time of the Cuban revolution in 1959, Soviet Third World
policy under Khrushchev – and ideological formulations of the
revolutionary process – had changed radically from the tight bipolar
and rigid Stalinist policy of the previous decade. Khrushchev
outlined these changes in his speech to the Twentieth Party Congress
in 1956. He made it clear that thenceforth the Soviet Union would
court the newly independent states in the Third World in order to
assist their development towards a non-capitalist path, and he
acknowledged that a peaceful road to socialism was possible.[1] These
were important innovations which had a direct impact on Soviet
reactions to the Cuban revolution. The Soviet Union had broken
out of its isolation, altered its ideological formulations towards a
more positive assessment of the role of the national bourgeoisie, and
embarked upon a foreign policy with a global reach. In the context
of the historical competition between the capitalist and socialist
systems, the conduct of Soviet foreign policy was openly designed to
'buy' influence in the Third World at the expense of the United
States and the former colonial powers in Europe. These policies were
not always mutually economically advantageous; on the contrary,
they often proved to be very costly to the Soviet economy. In order
to understand the development of Soviet-Cuban relations after
Khrushchev's ouster from the Kremlin in 1964, the period when the

links between the two states were first formed must be taken into account. I will come back to the significance of this for future Soviet policy in the concluding chapter.

The initial positive Soviet response to post-Batista Cuba was tempered with a certain amount of scepticism and caution regarding the revolution's orientation (given the unknown quality of Castro) and its long-term viability (given Cuba's proximity to the United States). The first tentative move to re-establish diplomatic relations between the two countries (broken by Batista in 1953) was made by the Soviet Union just two days after Castro's triumphant entry into Havana, at the head of his guerrilla army, on 8 January 1959.[2]

However, Fidel Castro was first and foremost a Cuban nationalist, and his heroes and role models were other Cuban (and Latin American) nationalists who had fought against Spanish colonialism and, later, US hegemony. He did not conduct his guerrilla struggle in the name of Marx, Engels or Lenin, but in that of Bolivar, Maceo and Marti. He had already stated at a Rotary Club lunch in Havana in January 1959 – attended by American and Cuban businessmen – that he was not a communist,[3] and he reiterated this during his visit to Washington three months later when he claimed to be opposed to all kinds of dictators, and 'that is why we are against communism'.[4] At this same press conference Castro told his audience that Cuba had not received any aid from the Soviet Union and had not requested any; furthermore, he intended to keep Cuba equidistant between the superpowers, although in the context of the global Cold War his heart was 'with the West'.

Fidel was a Cubanist, a Latin Americanist, a patriot and a nationalist who wished to establish a more equitable economic and political relationship with the United States, Cuba's traditional and most natural market. Yet the economic aims of the revolution challenged the structure of the regional system in Latin America, which had been dominated since the turn of the century by the intrusive power in the north. Plans for land reform and nationalization were bound to affect US economic interests, and an independent or non-aligned foreign policy challenged US political hegemony in the Western hemisphere. The Cuban revolution was bound to lead to tensions with the United States, and the outcome depended on the actions of both sides. Meanwhile, the Soviet Union's Third World policy under Khrushchev sought to take advantage of the contradictions between national revolutionary states and US 'imperialism'. As Castro's overtures to the United States were not reciprocated, Moscow's overtures to Havana became increasingly attractive.

The USA's self-fulfilling prophecy

Castro apparently feared that the Popular Socialist Party (PSP) posed a threat to his leadership and, in May 1959, just one day before the Agrarian Reform Law was announced (which brought the large estates into public ownership), the daily organ of the 26 July Movement, *Revolución*, openly denounced the communists for seeking to undermine Castro's position.[5] Earlier that same month *Revolución* questioned the reliability and trustworthiness of the communists, recalling their earlier participation in a government headed by the arch enemy Batista.[6] Then Fidel in person, in a nationwide television address, referred to the communists as counter-revolutionaries.[7] The PSP leadership responded to these attacks with caution, arguing that creating a rift between the 26 July Movement and the communists only served the interests of external forces intent on undermining the revolution.[8] During the May Plenum of the party, PSP General Secretary Blas Roca (who in the 1930s had helped in the construction of the Moscow metro) warned Castro against strengthening the real counter-revolutionary forces in the United States by attacking the communists.[9]

This first crisis between the Fidelistas and the communists soon resolved itself as a result of internal and external pressures arising from opposition to the Agrarian Reform Law. The negative reaction in the United States helped to polarize the factions in Cuba, to harden Fidel's attitude against those who opposed the reform and to soften his views towards the PSP, which supported it. It was not a question of his suddenly becoming sympathetic to Marxism-Leninism (that was to come later), but one of national pride and survival in the face of an increasing threat from the United States. It was an ideal situation for Kruschchev's Third World strategy to exploit.

As relations with the United States deteriorated during the course of 1959, Castro came to recognize the importance of the Soviet Union as a potential guarantor of Cuban national security. The first bilateral trade agreement was concluded in October, when the Soviet Union undertook to purchase 300,000 tons of Cuban sugar. However, this was not a new departure. The Soviet Union had been purchasing sugar from Batista for the previous four years, despite the absence of formal diplomatic relations. In fact, Cuba sold less sugar to the Soviet Union in 1959 than the average yearly sales between 1955 and 1958, even though the 1959 sugar harvest was the largest for nine years and demand in the Soviet Union was increasing.[10] Nevertheless, with the prospect looming of a cut in the US sugar quota, it was essential that an alternative market was found. In February 1960, in the first high-level visit of a Soviet official to Cuba, Deputy Prime Minister Anastas Mikoyan opened a Soviet trade fair in Havana, and signed one agreement providing credits of $100 million and a trade agreement for the purchase of Cuban sugar.[11]

The trade and aid agreement of 13 February 1960 marked a watershed in Soviet-Cuban relations. The USSR agreed to purchase 425,000 tons of sugar that year and one million tons annually for the following four years. Eighty per cent of the purchase was to be paid in Soviet merchandise and the remaining 20 per cent in hard currency.[12] There is no doubt that Castro would have preferred to sell surplus sugar to the United States, but he was forced to find alternative markets. The agreement with the Soviet Union was the logical outcome of US policies. The United States had sought to influence Castro by inflicting punishments in the form of economic warfare, whereas the Soviet Union was seeking to gain influence over Cuba by offering economic rewards. Castro was in a position to maintain his independent credentials at this stage by taking advantage of the Soviet card. However, changing one dependent relationship for another involved the risk of future Soviet leverage over the conduct of Cuban policy, a question I take up later.

Part of the 80 per cent payment for Cuban sugar in the February agreement was to be made up of Soviet oil deliveries. This was of great advantage to the Cubans, who owed $50 million to US and British oil companies, since a sugar/oil exchange enabled Castro to gain sufficient supply without spending precious and depleting financial reserves.[13] However, the oil companies in Cuba, in collaboration with the US government, refused to refine Soviet crude oil, thus forcing Castro's hand: the refineries were nationalized. The United States had hoped that the refusal to refine Soviet crude would precipitate a domestic crisis and ultimately lead to a moderation in Cuban policy. President Eisenhower went on to cut the Cuban sugar quota on 6 July 1960 in an open and deliberate attempt to undermine Castro's power. But the Soviet Union once more stepped into the breach. Within two weeks it had agreed to purchase 700,000 tons of sugar, the exact amount cut by Congress. A joint communiqué on the restoration of Soviet-Cuban diplomatic relations was signed on 8 May 1960. Cuba had turned to the East out of necessity; the Soviet Union turned to the Third World and assisted Castro out of political and strategic self-interest.

Although Khrushchev shared Castro's interest in preserving the territorial integrity and national security of the Cuban state, the two leaders' perceptions of the fundamental issues in global politics, including the significance of the Cuban revolution, were radically different. This perception gap inevitably led to different foreign policy priorities and strategies. For Castro, Latin American and Third World underdevelopment, economic dependency and imperialist domination were the central issues of global politics. For Khrushchev, the key issue was the competition between socialism and imperialism; developments in the Third World were seen in the context of the shifting correlation of forces and the changing strategic balance of power between East and West. From Castro's North-South perspective – and as the United States became increasingly hostile – it became impossible to compromise with the 'imperialists' and vital to assist other guerrilla movements in their struggle for liberation. From Khrushchev's East-West perspective, the increasing danger of mutual nuclear suicide made accommodation with the 'imperialists' desirable; the duty of the communist was to assist the Soviet Union in its historic competition, but without risking a US-Soviet confrontation. Given these basic premises, it is not surprising that Castro's theory of revolution and active policy of aiding Latin American guerrilla movements ran directly counter to Khrushchev's theory of peaceful coexistence and active policy of seeking accommodation with the United States. This conflict of interests was to increase in intensity in the post-Khrushchev era.

Castro's conversion to Marxism-Leninism
The domestic political process in the United States seems to have institutionalized and legitimized what can perhaps best be termed a Cold War belief system, with its operating symbols of 'democracy' versus 'totalitarianism'. The presidential campaign of 1960 accordingly saw Kennedy and Nixon battling with each other to convince

public opinion that they would take the toughest stand against this new communist menace to stability in the hemisphere. The election campaign itself thus succeeded in reinforcing anti-Castro attitudes and in hardening US policy. As two American scholars put it, 'the one concrete result of the campaign was the Eisenhower administration's imposition on Cuba of an economic embargo – perhaps more in an attempt to bolster Mr Nixon's political campaign than to accomplish a defined purpose in our national interest'.[14] The embargo, declared on 19 October 1960, was followed a week later by the nationalization of all remaining US property in Cuba.

By the time of the US-supported Bay of Pigs invasion in April 1961, Cuba was totally dependent on the Soviet Union for its oil imports, and as the economic embargo took effect, the Cuban economy became reoriented towards dependence on the USSR. A succession of US policies had produced a self-fulfilling prophecy. The fear of a US military intervention was the last straw for Castro: as the invasion force was making its final preparations for a landing, he declared that the Cuban revolution was 'socialist' in nature.

Castro had been seeking a Soviet security guarantee in the event of military hostilities from the United States since the previous summer, and perhaps by announcing his socialist credentials on the eve of the Bay of Pigs invasion he hoped to persuade Moscow to provide assistance. Although the Soviet Union hoped to gain influence in global politics as a result of the contradictions between the United States and the less developed countries, it did not wish to risk a direct military confrontation between the superpowers. Nevertheless, following the shooting down of the U-2 spy plane over the Soviet Union in May 1960 and the subsequent collapse of summitry and the 'spirit of Camp David', Khrushchev did make some ambiguous declarations of support for Cuba in the event of external aggression. In a speech to the All-Union Teachers' Congress in July, the Soviet leader told the delegates that 'figuratively speaking, in case of need, Soviet artillerymen can assist the Cuban people with their rocket fire should aggressive forces in the Pentagon dare to start an intervention against Cuba'.[15]

The Cubans sought to obtain a more explicit guarantee of Soviet military support than that contained in Khrushchev's statement, fearing that his overriding concern with peaceful coexistence, East-West relations, the strategic balance and the danger of nuclear war meant that in effect Cuba stood alone. This was not forthcoming, and even though both Castro and the Cuban press professed to view Khrushchev's words as an undertaking to use nuclear missiles against the United States if it did attack Cuba,[16] Soviet media coverage never interpreted the statement as an explicit commitment to defend the island.[17] Khrushchev's statement, like many others he made, proved to be an embarrassment to the rest of the political elite. In keeping with the Soviet tradition of rewriting history, official versions of his speech omit the reference to rockets.

In the event direct Soviet military assistance was not required to defeat the CIA-directed landing at the Bay of Pigs in April 1961. Yet the invasion did highlight the vulnerability of Cuban national security to any future US-sponsored military intervention, and hence the necessity to build up the Revolutionary Armed Forces. Castro had sought to maintain neutrality in the East-West conflict, but following the Bay of Pigs fiasco he quickly stressed his allegiance first to socialism and, within a few months, to that form of socialism practised in the Soviet Union. On 2 December 1961, in a most important speech to the Cuban people, he stated that he was a Marxist-Leninist, and that whereas earlier his heart had been with the West in the Cold War, it was now firmly with the East.[18] Of course many observers in the United States had been claiming that Castro was a communist from the start, but the most likely explanation for Castro's statement in December 1961 was his desire to increase pressure on Moscow to strengthen its commitment to Cuba in response to US antagonism and the very real threat to the revolution. Castro's earlier (and later) conflicts with the PSP indicate clearly that he came only late and reluctantly to the communist fold. He took over the communists, not the other way around. Four months after his speech the Soviet Union officially endorsed Cuba's socialist path of development, thereby – in theory at least – increasing its internationalist duty to defend the revolution.[19] Indeed, it now began to intensify its military aid to Cuba.

The missile crisis
Khrushchev states in his memoirs that the subject of Cuba was frequently on the Politburo agenda at this time and that 'we had an obligation to do everything in our power to protect Cuba's existence as a socialist country and as a working example to the other countries in Latin America'. In order to help bolster Castro's

defences Khrushchev supplied him with 'as many arms as the Cuban army could absorb', but still there was a danger of a US invasion.[20] Khrushchev maintains that the 'fate of Cuba and the maintenance of Soviet prestige in that part of the world preoccupied me even when I was busy conducting the affairs of state in Moscow and travelling to the other fraternal countries', and that when in Bulgaria 'one thought kept hammering away at my brain: what will happen if we lose Cuba? . . . It would gravely diminish our stature throughout the world, but especially in Latin America.' Thus, in order to establish an effective deterrent to US aggression, 'the logical answer was missiles'.[21]   According to Khrushchev, the decision to install missiles in Cuba was his own, it was later carefully considered by the 'collective', and it was taken in order to ensure Cuban security and Soviet prestige. Khrushchev maintains that when he put the idea to Castro the two leaders 'argued and argued. Our argument was very heated. But, in the end, Fidel agreed with me.'[22] Castro has confirmed that the initiative came from Moscow, that it had surprised him, and that at first it had not seemed the most effective way to enhance Cuban security.[23]

It is very unlikely, despite what Khrushchev claims in his memoirs, that his motivations were concerned with Cuban security, even if the establishment of Soviet missiles on the island would have served Cuban interests. His primary concern was in fact the overall strategic balance of forces. By secretly placing missiles in Cuba, a secret he possibly kept from many of his colleagues in the leadership, he hoped to redress the imbalance in strategic forces between the United States and the Soviet Union. The USSR persuaded the Cubans to request the missiles, took steps to ensure that they would be completely under Moscow's control, and then made an agreement with the United States to remove them, without consulting Castro.

The whole episode was a major humiliation for the Cuban leader and led to a serious rift in Soviet-Cuban relations. Khrushchev states that although Soviet-US relations improved soon after the crisis, 'our relations with Cuba . . . took a sudden turn for the worse. Castro even stopped receiving our ambassador.'[24] In order to overcome the strains, Mikoyan was sent to Cuba on 2 November 1962 and stayed there for over three weeks, even though his wife was dying in Moscow. He was not given a warm welcome in Havana, but he did prevent a rupture in relations. However, this was gained at a price, as evidenced by the favourable terms of the new trade agreement signed two months later, in which the Soviet Union increased its payments for Cuban sugar and agreed to provide more aid for economic development.

The Cubans had in this respect turned the situation to their advantage. But the missile crisis had a number of important lessons for them: first, it demonstrated that US hostility to the revolution was implacable; second, it proved that ultimately Cuba stood alone in meeting this hostility; third, it gave further evidence that Moscow was more concerned with peaceful coexistence and accommodation with its enemies than with supporting its friends; and, finally, it convinced Castro that he should do all in his power to ensure Cuban autonomy. As he put it, 'Never again in the chess game of power' would Cuba be in the position of 'playing the docile pawn'.[25]

The development of Soviet-Cuban relations was largely the product of US hostility to Castro, Khruschev's new Third World policy and Cuban economic requirements. However, there were always strains in the relationship, because of the differing conceptions in Moscow and Havana of the nature of global politics. These strains increased in intensity during the course of the 1960s, with the missile crisis especially serving to exacerbate them. Foreign Minister Gromyko's speech to the session of the USSR Supreme Soviet which discussed the October crisis stressed how closely intertwined the destiny of the world was with Soviet-US relations, and how this fact demonstrated the necessity for peaceful coexistence.[26] An important *Pravda* editorial in January 1963 took up this theme, stating that the most important issue in world politics was ensuring the maintenance of peace. The editorial was an open counter-attack on Albania (and by implication China), which had interpreted Khrushchev's agreement with Kennedy as an act of cowardice and regarded peaceful coexistence as a 'sell-out' to imperialism. Castro shared these views, and the editorial was directed as much at him as at the other wayward socialist states when it declared that it was not possible to reach communism through a thermonuclear war.[27]

Running through the deputies' speeches at the Supreme Soviet session was a notable streak of hurt pride and anger at any accusation that the Soviet Union lacked firmness and courage after the experiences of World War II. The resolution of the missile crisis was portrayed in Moscow as an example of peaceful coexistence in action, the outcome of which reinforced Cuba's sovereignty and independence in so far as the United States, for the first time ever, had agreed not to mount an attack on the island. This has of course proved to be true, for the Khrushchev/Kennedy agreement has formed the basis for Cuban security against US military intervention. For Castro, though, the significant and humiliating factor was that he was not party to the agreement – and officially Cuba still does not recognize it.

3

SOVIET PRAGMATISM UNDER BREZHNEV

The new Soviet leadership under Leonid Brezhnev was confronted with a dilemma in its foreign policy goals: how to maintain its revolutionary credentials in the Third World in the face of a Chinese challenge to its leadership of the communist world, while at the same time establishing relations with non-revolutionary governments. In December 1964 the Soviet Union sought to overcome these inter-related problems by convening a Conference of Communist Parties in Havana. As W. Raymond Duncan documents, the objectives of the Soviet-inspired conference were threefold: first, to isolate China and ensure Moscow's supremacy in the Third World communist movement by excluding pro-Chinese groups from the conference; second, to encourage Cuba to side with the USSR in the Sino-Soviet conflict; and, third, to moderate Castro's stress on armed struggle and thus prevent a split among the Latin American communist parties.[1] In the event a compromise was reached whereby the Soviet Union and Cuba both agreed to recognize the validity of each other's strategy, with the path chosen (i.e., armed struggle or peaceful change) dependent upon the objective circumstances prevailing in a particular country. In a sense this was a victory for Castro, who studiously avoided direct criticism of Beijing, did not acknowledge Moscow's leadership of the Latin American communist movement, and succeeded in gaining at least partial legitimacy from the Soviet Union for his own theory of armed revolutionary struggle. Furthermore, he openly opposed the negotiations the superpowers had been engaged in, since the missile crisis, which were leading to the establishment of the Hot Line and the Partial Test Ban Treaty. Castro was certainly no one's pawn, despite increasing economic dependence on the Soviet Union.

The Havana compromise was not to last long, since Castro's belief in the efficacy of armed struggle against imperialism was strengthened by two events in the first half of 1965. When the United States began bombing North Vietnam in February, Castro made a strong call for international socialist solidarity. He called explicitly upon the Soviet Union to stand by its ideals and render all the support it could to counter US aggression, 'taking whatever risks may be necessary for Vietnam'. In the same speech he stressed the independence of Cuba's foreign policy, stating that 'we are not anyone's satellite, and we never shall be!'[2] When, two months later, 23,000 US troops landed in the Dominican Republic, the lesson for Castro was clear: the socialist bloc must support armed struggle against imperialism as the *only* way to gain liberation. The lesson for Moscow was radically different: support for guerrilla warfare not only challenged classical Marxist-Leninist ideology, which stressed the role of the vanguard communist party; it was also unsuccessful and risked an increase in tensions between the superpowers.

Moscow's foreign policy priorities were set out in a *Pravda* editorial in August 1965.[3] Once more the stress was on the peaceful coexistence of states with different social systems. There was no reference to supporting armed revolutionary struggle, although the Soviet Union's commitment to defend revolutionary gains against counter-revolution was a constant theme in the Brezhnev era. Castro, on the other hand, was intent on asserting his own independence in formulating Cuba's foreign policy, pointing out that his adherence to Marxism-Leninism did not imply that he had to abide by strictures emanating from Moscow. Marxism, he argued, was not a single 'religious doctrine, with its Rome, its Pope, and Ecumenical Council'.[4] In effect he was challenging Moscow (Rome), Brezhnev (the Pope) and the Soviet Politburo (the Ecumenical Council) for leadership of the revolutionary movement in the Third World, since he too had a single doctrine that he thought should apply universally and which, significantly, was in direct opposition to that advocated in the Soviet Union.

With similar objectives to those it had had for the Havana conference of 1964, the Soviet Union instigated the convening of the Tricontinental Conference in Havana in 1966. China's challenge to

Soviet hegemony over the international communist movement was mainly in the Third World, and the Afro-Asian People's Solidarity Organization (AAPSO) was a principal forum in which this challenge was being mounted. The Tricontinental Conference was designed to create a new Afro-Asian-Latin American People's Solidarity Organization which, with the inclusion of pro-Soviet Latin American groups, would have tipped the balance in Moscow's favour in its competition with Beijing. The Soviet Union also hoped that the conference would modify Cuban support for armed struggle. Neither of these designs was realized. The host nation drew up the invitations for other Latin American participants, and, as a result, only three pro-Moscow communist parties headed delegations to the Tricontinental Conference as opposed to twenty-three at the 1964 conference.[5] Castro, meanwhile, found his most natural place and role in international affairs at this gathering of Third World anti-imperialist states, and it is indicative of his North-South perspective that he used his position as chairman of the conference to promote Third World nationalist interests over those of the international communist movement. As Carla Anne Robbins puts it in her excellent study, 'Castro used his power to promote Havana's interests over Moscow's.'[6]

On the question of the appropriate revolutionary strategy for the Third World, Castro came out strongly in favour of armed struggle, a position endorsed by the majority of delegates and incorporated in the conference's final resolutions. One positive outcome for the Soviet leadership, however, was the attack Castro launched on the Chinese for attempting to interfere in Cuban domestic politics and for cutting rice supplies to Cuba. By breaking with Beijing Castro was of course helping to guarantee continued Soviet aid, but the Chinese threat to his own emerging position as the leader of the revolutionary movement in the Third World was also a factor in the split.

Cuba's challenge to Soviet interests

Castro's independent foreign policy in the Third World was a direct challenge to Soviet interests. The Brezhnev leadership's policy of forging economic links with Latin American governments for mutual advantage was threatened by its association with a revolutionary power that was seeking to overthrow them. In addition,

Castro was both challenging Moscow's title as the principal advocate of national liberation movements and undermining the influence of pro-Moscow communist parties in Latin America. Given the USSR's growing interest in accommodation with the United States in order to gain, among other things, Western technology, arms control agreements and stability in Europe, Castro's radical Third World policy ran counter to major Soviet policy goals. Nor were all internal Cuban developments to the satisfaction of Moscow. The Soviet Union was critical of many of Castro's economic policies in the 1960s: his emphasis on industrialization in the early years of the revolution; his promotion of moral, as opposed to economic, incentives to increase production; and the 'revolutionary offensive' to create 'genuine communism'. As Edward Gonzalez states, by the time that the new Communist Party of Cuba (PCC) was established in October 1965, 'the ascendancy of the Fidelistas over the party apparatus was virtually completed'.[7]

Between 1966 and 1968 Castro's challenge to the Soviet Union's ideological leadership in the Third World and to Soviet foreign-policy goals intensified. In 1966 he openly criticized Moscow for fostering diplomatic relations with the Frei regime in Chile and for giving economic aid to Brazil, claiming these were the actions of an 'accomplice of imperialism'. In 1967 he attacked the pro-Soviet communist parties in Latin America which supported the peaceful road to socialism, stating that 'those who are not revolutionary fighters cannot be called communists'.[8] His most strident condemnation was reserved for the Venezuelan Communist Party, the leaders of which he referred to as 'renegades', 'defeatists' and 'capitulators' who had sold out to the 'pro-imperialist oligarchy': 'As for us, we are Marxist-Leninist; let others do as they please. We will never re-establish relations with such a government.' Castro was in effect attacking the Soviet Union, and in order to counter any thought in Moscow about bringing him to heel, he went on in the strongest of terms to proclaim his independence: 'We proclaim it to the world: this Revolution will hold true to its path; this Revolution will follow its own line; this Revolution will never be anybody's satellite or yes-man. It will never ask anybody's permission to maintain its own position either in matters of ideology, or on domestic or foreign affairs.'[9]

In June 1967 Prime Minister Kosygin led a twenty-person Soviet delegation to Havana to try and patch up the differences between the countries. But little of substance resulted from the 'summit meeting'. The CPSU has always been reluctant to air its dirty linen in public, whether in relation to internal party frictions, or to frictions between fraternal communist parties. *Tass* described Kosygin's talks with Castro as 'a frank exchange of opinions', without spelling out the disagreements indicated by this choice of words. Soviet attitudes can be deduced, however, from critical articles written by pro-Moscow Latin American communists in the Soviet press. It is significant, for example, that Luis Corvalán of the Chilean Communist Party, which advocated peaceful means to achieve socialism, should have been given space in *Pravda* to attack Castro's policies just after Kosygin's visit.[10] Yet the official Soviet response to what was really the strongest challenge to date to the leading role of the communist party in the revolutionary process was extremely mild.[11]

In Cuba, 1968 was named the Year of the Heroic Guerrilla. At a time when Moscow and Washington were making some moves towards a new detente relationship, the Cubans were advocating revolutionary violence for the black population in the United States, as well as for guerrillas in Africa, Asia and Latin America. In February 1968 Castro once more turned his attention to an internal challenge to his leadership from a group of old pro-Soviet communists. Anibal Escalante was at the centre of the storm. After being earlier purged for seeking to take over the newly established Integrated Revolutionary Organizations (ORI) in 1962, Escalante had spent three years in exile in Czechoslovakia. Now he was charged with heading a so-called 'microfaction', consisting almost entirely of former members of the PSP, which allegedly was plotting treason against the Cuban revolution. At a specially convened Central Committee meeting, Escalante was said to have planned to create a deterioration in Cuba's situation so that the Soviet Union could intervene in a 'friendly way', thus facilitating his own ascendancy to power. Escalante had close contacts with officials from the Soviet embassy and made frequent trips to Moscow, where his daughter was attending the Moscow Conservatory of Music. The criticisms levelled against the microfaction could equally well have been made against the CPSU;[12] indeed, by implication, Moscow was also in the dock.

The charges included: (1) advocating giving up Cuba's independent line and granting Moscow undisputed leadership of the international communist movement; (2) criticizing Castro's 'one-man show'; (3) stressing the role of orthodox communist parties, rather than revolutionary guerrilla movements, in Latin America; (4) criticizing the Communist Party of Cuba for not acting in accordance with Leninist principles, its lack of a collective leadership, the irregularity of Politburo and Central Committee meetings and its undermining of democratic centralism; (5) praising Khrushchev's removal of missiles from Cuba in 1962; and (6) attacking Che Guevara. In his report to the Central Committee, Fidel Castro's brother, Raúl, said of the microfaction: 'They even went so far as to aspire to the application of political and economic pressure by the Soviet Union to force the Revolution to draw closer to that country.'[13] This, of course, is exactly what happened!

Moscow asserts its influence over Havana
It is evident that the USSR had indeed initiated economic pressures from late 1967 in order to gain Cuban compliance with Soviet ideological and foreign-policy goals. Although Moscow did not actually cut back on its aid to Cuba, it did not increase its supplies of oil to the level requested by Castro and it was slow in reaching a new trade and aid agreement for 1968. But the Soviet leaders did not wish to push Castro into a position of choosing between forced compliance or going it alone, for they knew that his national pride would not allow him to give in to external demands, irrespective of the consequences. The United States had learned (or should have learned) this lesson to its cost, although even at this stage it failed to recognize, let alone exploit, the serious rift between Moscow and Havana. In resolving the missile crisis Kennedy had allowed Khrushchev to save some face, rather than placing him in a position which would have cost him domestic and international credibility and prestige. (It is interesting to note that no US president has shown a similar approach in dealing with Castro.) Similarly, Brezhnev recognized the need to tread carefully in his dealings with the Cuban nationalist. The Cuban revolution had not been imposed by Soviet tanks; nor was it possible to ensure Cuban compliance by resorting to East European-type armed intervention (given the proximity of the United States and the vast distance separating Moscow and Havana). However, the USSR had invested too many roubles and too much prestige to 'lose' Cuba or allow it to continue threatening Soviet positions and priorities.

During 1967 Cuba's oil requirements had risen by 8 per cent, while Soviet supplies rose by only 2 per cent, and in January 1968 Castro announced petrol rationing, stating that it was due to insufficient Soviet effort to keep Cuba adequately supplied.[14] At the same time as Moscow was effectively cutting oil supplies to Cuba, it was increasing its exports to Brazil and Argentina, two of the Latin American countries hostile to Castro. In his Central Committee speech documenting the microfaction's links with Soviet officials, Raúl Castro referred to a conversation between Rudolf P. Shliapnikov, Second Secretary in the Soviet embassy, and members of the microfaction, in which the Soviet diplomat pointed out that if Cuba was thinking of breaking with the USSR, 'all we have to do is tell the Cuban government that repairs are going to be made in the port of Baku that will last for three weeks'.[15] This clearly exaggerated Soviet leverage, but cutting back on oil supplies certainly did put pressure on Castro to moderate his revolutionary rhetoric at a time when Soviet priorities were to build a new detente relationship with the United States.

One thing that is not clear during this period is the extent to which, if at all, the Soviet Union was seeking to gain more influence in Cuba's domestic affairs through Escalante and the old communists. The Soviet press was fairly quiet on the whole affair, merely reporting the purge of the microfaction without comment or mention of the details.[16] However, it is not unlikely that the Soviet Union was seeking to influence internal politics through its contacts with trusted communists. There are striking parallels here with the intra-party conflict between Maurice Bishop and Bernard Coard in Grenada some fifteen years later. It is interesting to note that Castro strongly supported Bishop, the charismatic nationalist, rather than the hard-line pro-Soviet Marxist-Leninist, Bernard Coard. (Grenada is covered in detail in Chapter 7.)

At the same time as cutting back on its oil deliveries, the Soviet Union had deliberately drawn out the annual round of negotiations for the bilateral trade and aid agreement in an attempt to put more pressure on Castro. When the economic agreement for 1968 was finally signed, it called for an increase in trade 13 per cent below that of the previous year, and Castro made it plain that he saw this as a way of applying pressure on Cuba.[17] He was right, of course, and the general Western interpretation is that the pressure worked: Castro began to moderate his revolutionary rhetoric and accepted the Soviet invasion of Czechoslovakia in August 1968.

However, this interpretation overlooks certain facts which lead to a different conclusion. The purge of the microfaction occurred *after* the Soviet Union had begun to bring economic pressure to bear on Cuba, which indicates that Castro was reasserting his independence from Moscow rather than giving in to its demands. In February 1968 Cuba refused, despite Soviet entreaties, to attend the Consultative Meeting of Communist Parties in Budapest, which the Soviet Union had convened to restore its authority in the communist movement following the split with China. North Vietnam, North Korea, China and Albania also refused to send delegates. In April Cuba signed an agreement with Romania, whose delegation had walked out of the Budapest meeting, in which both sides were to cooperate in developing Cuba's oil resources. Finally, in May, Cuba denounced the Non-Proliferation Treaty then being discussed in the United Nations; Raúl Roa, the Foreign Minister, proclaimed that 'Cuba will never renounce its right to defend itself with weapons of any kind, whatever their nature'.[18]

Thus it is clear that despite Soviet economic pressure Castro did not fall into line with Moscow's attempt to enforce unity on the communist parties. He retained his North-South Third World credentials by opposing the Non-Proliferation Treaty, to which the Soviet Union attached great importance but which the Cubans considered to be an example of the strong against the weak; he reiterated his belief in armed struggle; and he condemned the USSR's advocacy of peaceful coexistence. In other words, at this time of unprecedented Soviet economic pressure, he took an ardently independent line. But then, in August 1968, came the Soviet-led invasion of Czechoslovakia.

There are differing interpretations in the West of Castro's attitude to the Soviet intervention in Czechoslovakia, but a general consensus exists that it somehow marked a watershed in Soviet-Cuban relations. The important point is that the Cuban leader did give Moscow his political backing for the invasion – perhaps reluctantly, yet less critically than Britain gave support to the USA when it later intervened in Grenada. However, it would be mistaken to view this as caving in to Soviet pressure. After all, here was Moscow tied up with a crisis in an area it perceived to be of vital geostrategic importance, and forced to take an action that was bound to have reverberations throughout the world. Cuba, some 6,000 miles away, was if anything in a position to assert influence on its patron in exchange for solidarity with the Soviet action. Indeed, the most likely explanation is that Cuba decided to support the Soviet Union at this moment of crisis because it was in its own political and security interests to do so. Castro publicly acknowledged that the sovereignty of the Czechoslovak state had been violated, yet he argued that the decision had been painful but necessary from the 'political point of view'.[19]

Castro justified the invasion in the name of international socialist solidarity against the intrigues of imperialism. He referred to Cuban students returning from Eastern Europe with stories of the local youth being influenced by ideas emanating from the West. Dubcek's socialism was seen in this light, and it was not something Castro would have allowed to develop in Havana. He was equally keen to see that it did not gain ground in Eastern Europe, and was genuinely in favour of stamping out what he saw as a dangerous capitalist orientation in Prague. He went on to ask rhetorically if the Warsaw Pact governments would abide by their internationalist duty and, in the event of imperialist aggression, come to the defence of Vietnam, North Korea or Cuba. Castro may have feared that the United States would respond to the Soviet invasion by instigating an attack on Cuba; he therefore wished to gain a stronger commitment from the Soviet Union that he could expect some assistance if this happened. The invasion may also have been seen in a positive light in Havana in so far as it jeopardized a superpower detente that threatened to undermine Soviet solidarity with revolutionary governments in the Third World.

Thus Castro had his own reasons for supporting the Soviet invasion, although it is true that he soon began to tone down some of his radical revolutionary statements, albeit without ever completely abandoning his strategy. This moderation is usually taken as evidence of Cuban capitulation to Soviet pressure, but again the story is more complex. The Soviet-Cuban relationship, as it developed in the late 1960s and early 1970s, did become far more cooperative and cohesive – but this was due as much to changing domestic, regional and international realities as to any Soviet use of coercive power. Although Castro was full of praise for Che Guevara, the death of the international revolutionary in the Bolivian jungle had led to a reappraisal among the Fidelistas of the Cuban guerrilla strategy in Latin America. Che's death symbolized the collapse of the revolutionary movement in Latin America which, by the end of the 1960s, was virtually destroyed. There was little use in continuing a policy destined to fail.[20] The Cuban leadership came to realize that they had perhaps been too optimistic in their assessments of the potential for radical revolutionary change in Latin America, and that seeking to export revolution where the conditions were not ripe, most clearly in Bolivia and Venezuela, alienated Cuba from its fellow Latin Americans and isolated it completely in the Western hemisphere. In addition, the emergence of a radical leftist military regime in Peru in October 1968 helped to change the Cuban view of inter-American relations, and led to a shift in policy, which now became more pragmatic.

Another important factor leading to this reassessment of Cuban policies was the domestic economic situation, which looked decidedly bleak towards the end of the 1960s. Cuba therefore had very good reasons during this period to moderate its policy towards Latin America, and the seemingly rapid switch to accommodation with the Soviet Union actually served Cuban as much as Soviet interests. This emerging cooperative relationship set the pattern for Soviet-Cuban relations into the 1970s, a relationship in which the poor Third World client had a certain amount of influence over its superpower patron.[21]

4
THE INSTITUTIONALIZATION OF THE RELATIONSHIP

In the 1970s Cuba still maintained an independent position on certain questions of revolutionary strategy, but Soviet-Cuban relations were now marked by a tight cooperation which served the interests of both states. Castro's support for the Soviet invasion of Czechoslovakia was repaid the following summer, when the Soviet Union answered his call for a greater show of solidarity with the Cuban revolution. In July 1969 a flotilla of Soviet warships visited Havana, the first time in history that a Soviet warship had entered the port of a Latin American city. This was an important gesture, demonstrating that Soviet capabilities could be deployed in defence of a distant socialist ally. Foreign Minister Gromyko, at a meeting of the Supreme Soviet that same month, had stressed that the USSR would do 'everything to assist the Cuban Republic and its people to overcome pressures and provocations'. In November Defence Minister Grechko spent a week in Cuba 'in response to an invitation extended by Major Raúl Castro, Minister of the Revolutionary Armed Forces'.[1] Raúl had talks with Grechko in Moscow six months later, and then with Brezhnev in October 1970. It has been suggested that Raúl had sought during these meetings to gain Cuban membership of the Warsaw Treaty Organization, although no concrete evidence exists to substantiate such claims.[2] It is clear, though, that in the early 1970s the Soviet Union increased its military aid to the Cubans and began delivering more modern and sophisticated equipment, including, by the spring of 1972, MiG-23s for the Cuban air force.[3] This was of course also a time when Nixon and Brezhnev were engaged in the most ambitious postwar attempt yet to improve superpower relations; then, in the autumn of 1970, the emerging detente process was put at risk as a result of a 'mini crisis' linked to Soviet naval activity in Cuba.

Cienfuegos

In September 1970 U-2 reconnaissance flights had discovered what appeared to be the construction of a permanent base for Soviet nuclear submarines in the deep-water bay at Cienfuegos. The *New York Times* argued that such a base 'would be the equivalent of installing land-based missiles as Russia attempted in 1962, then touching off a dramatic confrontation'.[4] This view was shared by the Nixon administration, and hence the issue became a test of the Kennedy/Khrushchev understanding of October 1962. Although some of Nixon's advisers, especially those in the Pentagon, advocated a confrontational response to force Moscow to desist, the President and his National Security Adviser, Henry Kissinger, sought to resolve the crisis through 'quiet diplomacy'. This time, in contrast to 1962, a crisis of major and frightening proportions was avoided; the Soviet Union again backed down and ceased construction of the base. Yet the Cienfuegos issue is interesting and important on a number of counts.

Castro had always been very suspicious of Nixon, who had been the first in the Eisenhower administration to advocate a military solution to the Cuban problem. In the summer of 1970 the Cubans became very worried that, as President, Nixon was now planning a direct military invasion of the island. In other words, it would have been very reassuring to Cuba if the Soviet Union could have obtained from Nixon a reaffirmation of the Khrushchev/Kennedy understanding, even if Castro did not publicly recognize it. In his memoirs Henry Kissinger relates how, the month before the Cienfuegos crisis, the Soviet Union through its embassy in Washington had sought to gain such a reaffirmation from Nixon.[5] Interpreting this request, Raymond Garthoff suggests that the USSR was seeking to gain official US recognition of the 1962 agreement in order to reassure Castro that his fears were groundless.[6] It is significant that when the Cienfuegos affair was finally settled by Moscow and Washington, with both sides publicly confirming their commitment to the 1962 agreement, Castro neither taunted Moscow with capitulation, nor criticized the Khrushchev/Kennedy agreement – even though the Cubans were again excluded from the diplomatic process.

Although Brezhnev decided to withdraw from Cienfuegos, the ships which had caused so much concern in Washington continued to operate in the Caribbean for a further four months, moving in and out of Cienfuegos and port-hopping along Cuba's coast. The US navy had been operating in the Black Sea for years, and with the growth in the Soviet fleet there was no reason why Soviet warships should not be able to enjoy the international right to sail in the Caribbean. This they continued to do, making frequent visits to Cuban ports, which must have given Castro a greater sense of security than he had had in October 1962.

Although the Soviet Union would not consider Cuban membership of the Warsaw Pact, Moscow's military commitment to Havana, even at a time of East-West detente, was stronger than ever. Both Castro and Brezhnev benefited from this new cooperative relationship, since Soviet and Cuban interests seemed to coincide in the 1970s to a greater extent than ever before. This is not to say that there were no contradictions at all between the two states, nor that Castro's basic North-South perspective had in any way weakened. Rather, the *essential* interests of both states in the early 1970s – domestic economic growth and national security – were the same, and therefore helped in the development of the very tight relationship which had materialized by 1975.

Economic integration into the Soviet bloc

Whereas Raúl had failed to attain his optimum goal during this period (membership of the Warsaw Pact), Carlos Rafael Rodríguez and Osvaldo Dorticos succeeded in attaining theirs (membership of the CMEA). Rodríguez was an 'old communist' from the PSP; Dorticos, President of the Republic, although not a former PSP member, was an economist whom the Soviet leadership trusted. Following the failure in 1970 to produce the much-publicized 'ten million ton' sugar harvest – the most serious blow to Castro's personal rule since the revolution – these two men were given the responsibilty of organizing the Cuban economy on a more sound footing. Rodríguez had said in April 1960 that the Cuban revolution was 'not going to be settled on the basis of the armed struggle . . . but more than all else, it has to be reasserted in the economic field'.[7] The collapse of guerrilla movements in Latin America and the parlous state of the Cuban economy made these words seem prophetic.

Talks between Brezhnev and Rodríguez in Moscow in January 1970 initiated a process of negotiation which culminated in Cuba's membership of the CMEA in 1972. Dorticos followed Rodríguez to Moscow, where he held talks with Brezhnev in April 1970, and Rodríguez was again in the Soviet capital in December that year, when an agreement was reached to establish a Cuban-Soviet Commission for Economic, Scientific and Technical Cooperation. The first session of the Cuban-Soviet Commission was held in Havana in September 1971. Baibakov, Chairman of the Soviet State Planning Agency, was in Havana in April 1971, and Prime Minister Kosygin paid his second visit to the Cuban capital in October, where he held talks with the Castro brothers, Dorticos and Rodríguez. When Dorticos returned to Moscow in December, he was met at the airport by all three leading personalities in the 'collective' leadership (Brezhnev, Podgorny and Kosygin), a clear indication of the status Cuba had achieved in Moscow's foreign relations.[8] This unprecedented series of high-level meetings culminated in July 1972 with the 26th Session of the CMEA, attended by Rodríguez, at which Cuba's application for membership was considered and 'unanimously approved'.[9] As far as the United States was concerned, the worst possible scenario had taken place, largely as a result of sustained US economic pressure against Castro's Cuba. The island was now to be tightly integrated into the socialist bloc's economic system, the first state outside Moscow's direct sphere of influence to gain CMEA membership.

Cuba's admission to the CMEA marked a watershed in Soviet-Cuban relations, for it signalled a degree of mutual commitment on *both* sides, as Article 1 of the CMEA Charter states, to the development of tight 'economic integration', cooperation in production and coordination of national economic planning. Since Castro's decision to join had far-reaching economic and political consequences, the following questions need to be asked: why did Cuba join; why did the Soviet Union agree to Cuban membership; what were the costs and benefits for both sides; and, most importantly in the context of this paper, did Cuba's membership increase Soviet influence over the conduct of Cuban foreign policy?

It has already been intimated that Cuba's reason for seeking membership was a logical outcome of its position in the global economy by the early 1970s. Unlike other distant Third World client states of the Soviet Union, its very economic survival was dependent on aid from Moscow. Because of the structure of the Cuban economy (the requirement for imported oil and the reliance on the export of sugar) and the US total embargo, Moscow had become Havana's largest trading partner. The volume of trade between the two countries increased from 160 million roubles in 1960 to more than a billion by 1970.[10] It has been estimated that by 1972 cumulative Soviet aid to Cuba (made up of direct grants, trade subsidies, free military equipment and the cost of Soviet technical and military advisers) had reached some $4 billion.[11]

Seeking membership of the CMEA was a rational decision for a number of reasons. As a less developed country with low industrial capacity, Cuba stood to gain long-term, guaranteed preferential treatment and developmental assistance as part of the CMEA Charter's objective of evening up the economic levels of member countries. By coordinating its economic plans within the multilateral forum of the Council, Cuba stood to benefit from economic and technical assistance from Eastern Europe, for example to develop its nickel industry. The CMEA does provide real benefits for its less developed members in the Third World (Mongolia and Vietnam as well as Cuba). Isidoro Malmierca, the Cuban Foreign Minister, is surely not exaggerating when he states that 'we are the only oil-importing country of the Third World which did not have the slightest energy crisis in the difficult years when countries which did not have their own natural energy resources were forced to import fuel at incredibly increased prices'.[12] Cuba's integration into the CMEA corresponded with the 'sovietization' of the domestic political economy, and although this may seem to be the price Castro had to pay for membership, it should not be forgotten that there were always strong forces in Havana which from the outset had advocated a Marxist-Leninist model of development.[13] Having purged Escalante and other old communists with close ties to Moscow, Castro in effect began to institute the policies and structural changes that they had long recommended.

All major Western studies on the subject agree that one of the basic motivations in Moscow was to increase Soviet influence over

Cuban economic development, although no consensus exists on the extent to which this has been achieved. However, the neat compartmentalizing of politics and economics runs the risk of overlooking important factors in an influence relationship. This is especially true in the case of a Marxist-Leninist system. It is not simply a matter of 'Cuban economic dependence equals Soviet influence'. After all, Cuba was economically dependent upon the Soviet Union before joining the CMEA. In a Marxist-Leninist system, however, politics and economics are closely interwined, or 'fused', to use Valerie Bunce's term, and the impact of this fusion is great, since '"high politics" is at the same time "high economics", hierarchy within the polity is coterminous with hierarchy in the economy'.[14] Thus, by incorporating Cuba into the institutional structures of the CMEA, and encouraging Cuban economic development on the Soviet model, Moscow was gaining multiple channels through which it could influence far more than Cuba's economic policies. Furthermore, membership of the CMEA necessarily involved the establishment of new economic organizations in Cuba, which resulted in the delegation of important aspects of decision-making away from Castro's personalistic leadership. Many of the elite groups that benefited were old communists with economic and technical experience. Thus Castro's power was undermined while, potentially at least, Moscow's influence increased.[15]

The Soviet leadership had long found it frustrating that Castro, a self-professed Marxist-Leninist, had not established the political structures of a Marxist-Leninist system. Cuba's entry into the CMEA was partly designed to encourage him to remodel Cuba's polity along Soviet lines, thus making the island a more reliable ally and one which would serve as an example to other Third World states. The Soviet Union wished to structure the already dependent relationship by integrating the Cuban economy into the institutions of the Council, thereby making it more difficult for Castro to undertake policies not to the liking of the Kremlin. In the early 1970s Prime Minister Kosygin seemed to link Cuba's entry into the CMEA with the necessity for further Soviet-type communist development.[16] During his 1974 visit to Havana, Brezhnev noted that although Cuba 'is not among the big countries as regards area and population ... in present day international life, she holds a big, and I would even say, outstanding place'.[17] The Soviet leadership's view of Cuba as a major propaganda prize in its ideological competition with the United States was another incentive to incorporate it into the 'socialist commonwealth'.

Yet at the same time Brezhnev's priority on his foreign-policy agenda was the improvement of political and economic relations with the United States. Castro's revolutionary rhetoric threatened to undermine this. So Cuban membership of the CMEA seemed likely to make Castro tone down his revolutionary fervour and accept US-Soviet detente – something which Brezhnev mentioned in his speech in Havana. In an article on Soviet-Cuban relations, Darusenkov noted that after the USSR increased its economic commitment to Castro, Cuba 'actively supported the measures taken by the USSR and ... approved the USSR-USA negotiations and the documents signed as a result of these'.[18] After Cuba's entry into the CMEA, Castro did indeed express at least token support for East-West detente, and began to restructure the political system on classical Soviet Marxist-Leninist lines.

Another advantageous outcome of Cuba's CMEA membership was that the Soviet Union could spread the burden of bailing out the Cuban economy more equally among the other East European states. Having committed itself so heavily to the survival of the Cuban revolution in the 1960s, the Soviet Union could not easily reduce its stake without losing credibility and prestige in the increasingly important Third World arena. It therefore hoped that, by guaranteeing the island's economic survival and according it status in the 'world socialist system', it would oblige Cuba to serve its interests in the Third World, both as a model for other countries to follow and as an active agent for furthering Soviet objectives. Events in the 1970s and 1980s, for many in the West, served to show just how successful this later Soviet design proved to be. According to one US scholar, Cuba began to 'act as an international mercenary in exchange for a subsidy variously estimated at between $10 and $12 million a day'.[19] However, this argument is far too simplistic, and those that make it ignore not only the fact that Moscow and Havana often happen to have similar views and priorities in the Third World, and thus 'cooperate' in order to gain mutual advantage, but also that at times the two sides disagree over policy in the Third World, and in such cases it is not necessarily Cuba which gives way to the Soviet Union.

The institutionalization of the relationship

Having now considered how the Soviet-Cuban relationship developed during the 1960s and early 1970s, I shall turn to the important question of Soviet influence over Cuban foreign policy in regional conflicts.

5

THE ANGOLAN CIVIL WAR, 1975–6

By September 1986 more than 200,000 Cubans had performed their 'internationalist duty' by serving some 10,000 kilometres from home in support of the Popular Movement for the Liberation of Angola (MPLA). At this date there were still over 40,000 Cuban military and civilian personnel in Angola.[1] Without the direct participation of Cuban combat troops during the height of the civil war, the MPLA would certainly not have emerged victorious in March 1976, and more than eleven years later Cuban troops are still necessary to ensure the survival of the regime in Luanda. For an underdeveloped Caribbean island with a population of only ten million people, this global activism is quite remarkable – and unprecedented in international politics. Cuba's decisive role in the Angolan civil war was interpreted in Washington, Beijing and South Africa as one drawn up for it in Moscow to further the geostrategic interests of the Soviet Union. Cuba was viewed as a Soviet 'puppet' or 'surrogate' acting in Africa as a 'hatchet man' to further Soviet expansionist ambitions.[2] However, those who make these claims ignore the earlier history of Cuban and Soviet policies in Africa and fail to provide adequate evidence to support the surrogate thesis.

It is important to note that Cuba's active policy in Africa did not begin with the Angolan civil war – though certainly this marked a large escalation – but can be traced back to the early 1960s. Indeed, in 1960, before diplomatic relations had been established with the Soviet Union, Cuba sent military and medical supplies to the Algerian Liberation Front (FLN). Whereas Cuba developed close ties with African liberation movements from the outset, the Soviet Union had traditionally preferred to forge links with communist parties. For example, it was most likely through the Portuguese Communist Party that Moscow first made contact with the MPLA in the early 1960s, or even late 1950s.[3] As already noted, during the early years of the Cuban revolution, the old communists in the PSP were not always in favour with the revolutionary leadership, and communist parties in Latin America were not the most natural allies for Castro and Guevara to foster. This had created problems between Moscow and Havana. Similarly, in Africa, the Soviets and the Cubans had different perspectives concerning the revolutionary process. In the Algerian struggle for independence, for example, Moscow was influenced more by the French and Algerian communist parties, whereas Cuba was more directly involved with the FLN.[4]

The bulk of Western writings on Cuba's international activity in the 1960s focused on Castro's attempts to 'export' revolution to other Latin American countries. Cuba's African policy, at least up until the Angolan civil war, was virtually ignored, despite the fact that Che Guevera had led some 200 Cubans in combat against Moise Tshombe in Congo-Brazzaville in 1965.[5] The most likely reason for this omission is that much of the scholarship on Cuba emanated from the United States, which at that time had very little interest in southern Africa but a great stake in Latin America. Moreover, many of those writing on Cuba were (and still are) Cuban émigrés working in US universities. Che Guevara's exploits in Bolivia, where he eventually met his death, were widely publicized, but his African adventures three years earlier were barely mentioned. Yet Guevara had stated in 1964 that 'Africa represents one, if not the most important battlefield against all forms of exploitation that exist in the world, against imperialism, colonialism and neo-colonialism'.[6] In Castro's North-South perspective wherever imperialism was threatened it was the duty of every true revolutionary to render internationalist solidarity and assistance to the progressive forces struggling for independence. Cuba put into practice what it preached, not only in Venezuela and Bolivia, but to a much greater extent in Algeria and Congo-Brazzaville. Right up to the MPLA victory in 1976, Cuba was consistent in its support for Neto, something which cannot be said of the Soviet Union, whose support wavered and depended not only on the balance of power between the rival factions in Angola and on the internal cohesiveness and viability of the movement, but also on the level of tension between East and West.

The fact that Moscow twice cut off aid to the MPLA, once in 1963 and again between 1972 and 1974, while Castro's support and aid were constant, highlights the differences at the time between Soviet and Cuban perceptions and objectives (which have been somewhat overlooked since the cooperative intervention of 1976). The majority of studies on the subject explain the two instances of Soviet cuts in aid as simply a rational response to a situation in which continuing supplies would have been a waste of resources. During this period the faction-fighting within the MPLA, between two groups headed by Daniel Chipenda (who eventually defected to the FNLA) and Agostinho Neto, was indeed a major factor undermining the Soviet commitment to the liberation movement. However, it should not be seen as the only one. Soviet strategic and security priorities have always differed from those of Cuba. In addition, the USSR had suffered a number of setbacks in Africa during the second half of the 1960s, when, despite its heavy economic commitments, a number of progressive regimes (in Ghana, Mali and Guinea) were replaced by pro-Western governments. These disappointments, coupled with an interest in improving economic ties with the West, led Moscow to reformulate its Third World strategy.

The period between May 1972 and June 1974 also saw an unprecedented series of superpower summits at which President Nixon and General-Secretary Brezhnev sought to establish a new code of conduct affecting not only arms control and bilateral relations, but also superpower behaviour in Third World conflicts. In signing the Basic Principles Agreement and the Agreement on the Prevention of Nuclear War, both sides agreed not to seek unilateral advantage in the event of a regional crisis, and to consult with one another if relations between countries not party to the agreements involved the risk of escalation into a superpower confrontation.[7]

This was the first time that the superpowers had come close to establishing a crisis prevention regime, or rules of conduct in the Third World, and this aspect of the new detente relationship was accorded far more significance in the Kremlin than it was in the White House. Having achieved rough strategic parity with the United States, the Soviet Union interpreted the signing of the two agreements as official recognition by the United States of the

USSR's equal status in the *political* sphere too, reflecting what Brezhnev referred to as 'the general change in the correlation of forces in the world arena'.[8] It was not very long, however, before these agreements were put to the test: first in the Middle East in October 1973, and then two years later in Angola. There is no general consensus in the West on the extent to which, if at all, the Soviet Union moderated its behaviour in these two conflicts in compliance with the agreements, but certainly Moscow was confronted with a dilemma in each case, as it sought to maintain both its influence in the regions and its improved relationship with the United States.[9] The Cuban leadership was free of any such dilemma, and this could help to explain its consistent commitment at a time when Soviet aid to the MPLA was being cut between 1972 and 1974.

By the early 1970s Soviet policy towards the Third World had become far less ideologically motivated as other interests came to dominate the foreign-policy agenda. Sub-Saharan Africa was of little geostrategic importance to the Soviet Union, and any involvement in the Angolan civil war, while offering obvious opportunities for furthering Soviet influence, carried the risk of undermining superpower detente if it became too active. Thus there was a strong incentive for the Soviet Union to moderate its policy in Angola in order to preserve its more important relationship with the United States. By contrast, Cuban motivations in giving assistance to the MPLA in 1975 were strongly ideological, as they had been ever since Guevara's meeting with Neto ten years earlier. Clearly Cuba had no strategic or economic benefits to gain, and if Castro was acting as a surrogate of the Soviet Union, there is absolutely no evidence to support this. As noted already, if influence is to be asserted some form of communication is necessary to indicate the action state A requires state B to perform. In the case of Angola there is no documentary evidence that the Soviet Union communicated to Castro a desire that Cuba undertake an action (i.e., the sending of combat troops) that it would not otherwise have taken. There is likewise no documentary evidence that either carrots or sticks, promises or threats, were employed to ensure compliance with Soviet wishes.

Perhaps one could argue that Cuba did not significantly modify its behaviour by sending troops to Angola in 1975–6 – Cubans had been fighting in various African conflicts for over ten years – and was acting no differently from before. Then do we have a case of 'reinforcement', in which the Soviet Union influenced Cuba to perpetuate this behaviour in Angola, only on a larger scale than hitherto? The answer must be no, for what evidence is available suggests that Cuba acted independently of the Soviet Union in the early stages of the war, and then not necessarily always in accordance with Soviet wishes. It was Moscow, not Havana, which moderated its behaviour, and Moscow which, after initial doubts, came round to accepting Havana's strategy in Angola – not the other way around. However, this should not be interpreted as Cuban influence over the Soviet Union; a number of intervening factors, particularly the actions of the United States, China and South Africa, explain Brezhnev's eventual cooperation with the Cubans. Ultimately, both the Soviet Union and Cuba stood to gain from cooperative intervention. Angola was a case of a convergence of interests, albeit from different perspectives (one North-South, the other East-West), without influence being employed. To illustrate this more clearly, I shall examine the events themselves.

When the Caetano dictatorship in Portugal collapsed in April 1974, there were three indigenous groups contending for power in Angola: the MPLA, the National Front for the Liberation of Angola (FNLA), and the National Union for the Total Independence of Angola (UNITA). Cuban and Soviet policies in Angola diverged: the Soviet Union cut off all aid to the MPLA, while Cuba continued to supply it with military advisers and equipment. In an action/reaction cycle, a number of external powers intervened in the civil war and transformed what was essentially a national struggle between tribal and ideological groups into a central component of the global East-West competition. Just two months after the coup in Lisbon, the Chinese began channelling arms and military advisers to the FNLA through Zaire, on Angola's northern border. Ever since Kennedy's presidency, the CIA had maintained contact with the leadership of the FNLA, and one month after the Chinese began sending arms through Zaire, the United States did the same, using the same route.

Meanwhile, the Soviet Union, having failed in its attempt to prevent the Arab attack on Israeli positions in 1973, had moderated its behaviour in the Middle East, during the course of the October war, in accordance with what it judged to be the principles of the superpower agreements on crisis prevention. In the event the United States succeeded, through Kissinger's 'exclusionary diplomacy', in reducing Soviet participation in the final resolution to what in effect was a symbolic role. As Kissinger himself notes, the USSR complained bitterly at being deliberately excluded from the peace process.[10] The Soviet leadership did not lose faith in detente as a means to avoid superpower confrontation, but at the same time the disappointment in the Middle East strengthened its resolve to play a more assertive role in Angola. It was also increasingly worried that US-Chinese collusion over Angola was designed to ensure an outcome to the conflict which would weaken the Soviet position. Thus, in October 1974, following the US and Chinese deliveries of arms to the FNLA, the Soviet Union began resupplying military equipment to the MPLA.

Yet at this stage external intervention was minimal, and there was still some hope of an orderly transfer of power once the Portuguese had finally withdrawn. In fact, Portuguese and regional African leaders were encouraging the three political groups to cooperate in a diplomatic solution to the conflict. These efforts led to a meeting in January 1975 between Neto, Roberto (of the FNLA), and Savimbi (the head of UNITA) in Alvor, Portugal. An agreement was reached to establish a transitional government representing all three groups. Elections were scheduled for October 1975, and in the interim the three guerrilla armies were to be integrated into a new single national army.

Given the differences between the three movements, the prospects of the Alvor Agreement being implemented were anyway very slim, but external forces encouraged continuation of the conflict. Nevertheless, the Soviet Union did give its support to the Alvor Agreement, and as the civil war escalated in the spring of 1975, Moscow stressed the need for unity and adherence to the coalition governmental structure, and criticized outsiders who were aiding any of the three groups.[11] The Cubans, on the other hand, while paying some lip-service to the agreement, were opposed to any power-sharing, and fully supported a post-independence Angola under the total control of the MPLA.[12] The Ford administration in the United States remained silent on the issue, but its attitude was made clear by a decision in January to award $300,000 in covert aid to the FNLA. Wayne Smith, a former official in the US foreign service and a leading expert on Cuba, states that Ford and Kissinger deliberately encouraged Roberto to launch an attack on the MPLA in March 1975, and encouraged President Mobutu of Zaire to support the

FNLA with his own regular troops.[13] Publicly, however, the United States at the time denied giving any assistance to the FNLA or encouraging Roberto and Mobutu to launch their joint offensive.

Even so, the Soviet Union and Cuba were well aware of the true situation and reacted accordingly, though at this stage still independently of one another. The Soviets consistently expressed an interest in working towards a diplomatic solution throughout the summer of 1975, but the Ford administration chose to ignore these overtures in the belief that they could engineer a victory for the FNLA which would exclude the more radical and socialist-oriented MPLA from any future government in Luanda. The Soviet Union's response to the US-backed offensive against the MPLA in March was to increase its shipment of arms to Neto. Cuba, meanwhile, following a meeting in May between Neto and Cuban Comandante Flavio Bravo in Brazzaville, agreed to send several hundred military instructors to assist the training of MPLA recruits. There is no evidence that Moscow and Havana, in making these decisions, were coordinating their actions.

By July the MPLA had succeeded in regaining the ground it had lost to its opponents, and the prospect of an MPLA government, following the date set for independence in November, looked likely. It was at this stage that the United States greatly increased its involvement to ensure that this did not occur: the 40 Committee awarded aid totalling $32 million to the FNLA and UNITA (which had now joined forces), and set up a programme of covert action under CIA control which involved the recruitment of mercenaries and the direct participation of CIA personnel on Angolan territory as 'military advisers'.[14] Following some minor military interventions earlier in the year, in August South African regular army units crossed the border to intervene directly in the Angolan civil war in support of FNLA/UNITA, first by setting up training bases, and later by participation in combat. A delegation from the MPLA travelled to Moscow that same month with a request for more arms and military advisers. Although Moscow was prepared to increase the shipment of arms, it was not willing to risk the dispatch of Soviet military personnel. The Soviet media was still calling for a political resolution to the conflict. A similar request to Havana received a more positive response: a high-level Cuban military delegation arrived in Luanda in late August, and the following month the first contingent of Cuban troops set sail for Angola.

Again, there is no evidence that the Soviet Union and Cuba collaborated or coordinated their policies at this stage. The Cuban decision to send military personnel and equipment was taken independently of the Soviet Union and in response to a direct request from the MPLA following the first intervention of troops from the region's major power, South Africa. The equipment and military personnel were transported the enormous distance under Cuba's own steam in two merchant ships and one training ship. These had to be rapidly modified for their new cargo: 480 military specialists, vehicles, communications equipment and some doctors. One month after this limited contingent arrived in Luanda, between 5,000 and 10,000 South African troops launched an invasion of Angola from the south, coinciding with a further incursion of Zairean troops in the north. According to informed US sources, the United States knew in advance of the South African invasion, and 'high officials' in Pretoria later acknowledged that there had been an 'understanding' between the two countries.[15]

By 3 November South African troops had penetrated 700 kilometres into Angola and were rapidly advancing towards the capital city. The conflict had now been transformed from a guerrilla struggle into a full-scale war against a professional foreign invading army, and the MPLA leadership sent out 'an urgent appeal for international solidarity'.[16] In what many consider to be a 'semi-official' version of events, Gabriel García Márquez states that on 5 November 'at a large and calm meeting, the leadership of the Communist Party of Cuba reached its decision without wavering. Contrary to numerous assertions, it was a sovereign and independent act by Cuba; the Soviet Union was informed not before, but after the decision had been made.'[17] The decision reached was to send Cuban combat troops to Angola to assist the MPLA in its struggle against the foreign invaders. In response to Chinese assertions that Cuba was acting as a surrogate of the Soviet Union, *Granma* angrily proclaimed that the decision to send troops had been made entirely independently and was consistent with Cuba's 'revolutionary internationalism', in contrast to the PRC's counter-revolutionary activity in support of the South African 'fascists' and US 'imperialists'.[18]

Fidel Castro, in a speech commemorating the fifteenth anniversary of the Bay of Pigs, took up this theme again, stating that 'Cuba alone bears responsibility for taking that decision. The USSR ...

never requested that a single Cuban be sent to that country. The USSR is extraordinarily respectful and careful in its relations with Cuba. A decision of that nature could only be made by our own party.'[19] One of the leading Soviet experts on Angola likewise stresses that Castro acted independently of Moscow, and denies that the Soviet leadership played any role in the decision to send Cuban troops to Angola.[20] It was even suggested to me by a senior scholar at Moscow's Institute of World Economy and International Relations (IMEMO) that had Castro consulted the Soviet leadership at the time, he would not necessarily have found it in agreement with the decision.[21]

The initial airlift of Cuban troops to Angola, which began on 7 November, was carried out in old Cuban converted freighters and obsolete commercial aeroplanes. It was only after the United States put pressure on Barbados and other countries to deny Cuba refuelling rights that the Soviet Union began to supply transport aircraft to the Cubans, beginning in January 1976. By this time there were already an estimated 6,000 Cubans in Angola, a number which was to increase to a peak of around 20,000 two months later. The Cubans clearly made the decisive difference in the eventual MPLA victory in mid-March.

It is a fact that, to quote Carlos Rafael Rodríguez at the Fifth Summit of the Non-Aligned Movement, 'Without the . . . determination of the Soviet government, the Angolan and Cuban fighters would have lacked the means with which they crushed the South African offensive and sent other forces fleeing.'[22] However, it is also a fact that Soviet support for the MPLA did waver at times both before and during the civil war, in contrast to the constant support rendered by the Cubans.

Brezhnev's major foreign-policy goal in the early 1970s was to establish a more cooperative relationship with the West in order, in part, to gain access to Western technology. At the height of the civil war in October, the Soviet media was still calling for a diplomatic solution. The Ford administration not only failed to respond but sent Kissinger to Beijing, an action which can only have increased Soviet suspicions of US designs. It was only when it was already too late, when large numbers of Cuban troops were committed, and when, on learning of US covert operations, Congress was about to block any further aid to Angola, that Ford eventually made a proposal to the Soviet Union on mutual withdrawal. This was on

9 December, and it is significant that the airlift of Cuban troops actually stopped from that date for a period of two weeks, suggesting that even at this stage Moscow was ready to negotiate.[23] However, any agreement which would have led to anything other than an MPLA government fully in power in Luanda would have been totally unacceptable to Neto, to Castro and, by now, to the majority of the Organization of African Unity. The Clark Amendment, passed by the US Senate on 19 December, cut off further aid and laid the path open to an easy victory for the Soviet- and Cuban-backed MPLA.

It is inconceivable that the Soviet Union could have realistically been expected to initiate a dialogue with President Ford under such circumstances. Yet the remarkable fact remains that Moscow did take the US president's proposal seriously – perhaps the clearest indication of all of the high value Brezhnev attached to detente. However, given the sequence of events and US behaviour in the Angolan civil war up to that point, together with the very favourable prospect of an MPLA victory, Brezhnev ultimately stood to lose far too much by now attempting to salvage diplomacy for the benefit of the United States. As Wayne Smith writes, 'Rather than proving that diplomacy is a weak tool in dealing with Moscow and Havana, the Angola case in fact demonstrates the exact opposite: the United States almost certainly would have been better off had it backed the Alvor Agreement and discussed the situation frankly with the Soviet Union, advising them that America intended to keep hands off and warning them that they should do the same.'[24] There were contradictions between the Soviet emphasis on detente and peaceful coexistence within an East-West perspective, and Cuba's ideological emphasis and North-South perspective. The United States failed in this instance to take advantage of these contradictions, and the lack of willingness of Ford and Kissinger to negotiate with the USSR from a position of equality helped to produce another self-fulfilling prophecy. This appears to be a general feature of US policy towards Cuba.

The Soviet Union attached far more importance to the events in Portugal in 1974 than it did to the situation in Angola. One important element that stimulated greater Soviet participation on the side of the MPLA was the perception in Moscow that the United States was colluding with China in aiding the other two groups in the conflict. Kissinger was in China in October 1975, and the following month *Pravda* expressed the fear that President Ford's scheduled visit to Beijing in December would involve a coordination of US and Chinese strategies in Angola.[25] This fear was probably exaggerated, but it was nonetheless real and acted as an important motivating force for Soviet policy. The Soviet Union perceived itself to be reacting to events in Angola, and did not wish to lose out to what were viewed as US and Chinese interventions. It recognized the damage that its actions in Angola were doing to superpower detente, but this was put down to the 'ruling circles' in the United States who, in their own self-interest, misconstrued Moscow's behaviour. This reasoning was forcefully expressed by Georgi Arbatov in a two-page article in *Pravda*.[26]

Although at the outset the Soviet Union and Cuba acted independently on Angola – to the extent that the most important decisions in Moscow and Havana were reached without direct coordination – in the closing stages of the conflict both sides found it advantageous to cooperate. This was the result of developments beyond the control of both states, as other external actors, particularly the United States and South Africa, intervened to change the course of events. Cuba's well-established relations with national liberation movements on the African continent went back to the early 1960s, and its policy and behaviour in Angola were consistent with previous policies and actions. Cuban objectives in Angola were essentially ideological, and it would be mistaken to underestimate Castro's commitment to international solidarity with Third World liberation movements struggling for 'independence from neo-colonialism'.[27] Castro would himself spend up to fourteen hours a day in the command room of his General Staff, following 'the course of battles with pins on minutely detailed wall-sized maps, keeping in constant touch with the MPLA high command on a battlefield where the time was six hours later'. It is further claimed that 'his absorption in the war was so intense and meticulous that he could quote any statistic relating to Angola as if it were Cuba itself, and he spoke of its towns, customs and peoples as if he had lived there all his life'.[28]

The Cuban leader would personally visit the harbour or the airport in Havana and speak with the Cuban troops as they set off for the war, in order to show his solidarity and revolutionary commitment to the cause in which his fellow countrymen were to risk their lives. The argument that Castro was sending Cuban troops to die for Soviet interests is absurd. Not only Castro's style but also his perceptions and goals can be contrasted with those of the Soviet leadership. Brezhnev's priorities and objectives were not based on any overall ideological commitment to promote revolution in Angola; rather, he wished to prevent a rupture in US-Soviet relations. Any interest the USSR had in Angola – and southern Africa generally was not a high priority – related to geostrategic considerations. By the end of 1975 there was a coincidence of interests between the Soviet Union and Cuba, but this was due to a complex action/reaction cycle and sequence of events which, had they produced a different outcome, would not necessarily have resulted in Cuban-Soviet cooperation. The two states reached the same foreign policy positions independently and with different objectives in mind.

However, during the past few years, Cuba and the Soviet Union have instituted a regular series of trilateral consultations with Angola so as to coordinate the actions of all three states on 'all aspects of policy in southern Africa'.[29] This level of coordination is tighter than that between the Soviet Union, Cuba and Ethiopia (no such trilateral body has been established with Addis Ababa), even though, in the case of the war in the Horn, Soviet-Cuban cooperation was much closer from the outset.

6

THE CONFLICT
IN THE HORN, 1977–8

By March 1978, just two years after Cuba's decisive involvement in the Angolan civil war, up to 15,000 Cubans had intervened in another African conflict. Once more, the intervention proved to be the key factor in the outcome. However, an analysis of Cuban and Soviet behaviour in the Horn of Africa during this period makes it clear that, in contrast to their involvement in Angola, the two socialist states coordinated their policies from the outset. What is not clear is the extent to which Cuba in this instance was more directly influenced by the Soviet Union in the conduct of the war. Certainly the perception among many Third World leaders, and not just Western policy-makers, was that Castro had now begun to be less an autonomous actor and more an instrument of Soviet strategic objectives. Again, because of the lack of documentary evidence, it is impossible to prove or refute this thesis conclusively. For example, there is no source that can be cited to show that the Soviet Union offered rewards or threatened punishments if Castro did or did not agree to send Cuban troops to the Ogaden.

The situation in the Horn was more complex than in Angola: first, the conflict was not a civil war between opposing ideological factions, but an inter-state war between two countries that advocated socialist development; second, Cuba's links with both regimes were of relatively recent origin, so that its involvement cannot be described as part of an incremental decision-making process; third, any historical link that Cuba did have was not with either of the two governments, but with the Marxist Eritrean People's Liberation

Front (EPLF), which was fighting for independence from Addis Ababa. The Soviet Union had already shown in Angola that it was capable of changing its policies in the light of circumstances, in order to ensure its strategic objectives; in the case of Eritrea, Cuba changed its behaviour too, although Castro did ultimately maintain an independent position on this issue which conflicted with Mengistu's and, to a lesser extent, with Brezhnev's.

In order to assess the Soviet-Cuban influence relationship in the Horn of Africa, it is necessary to review the sequence of events in the region and examine Soviet and Cuban perceptions and reactions to them. Apart from links with the Eritrean rebels from 1967, Cuba had no historical interests in the Horn before the socialist-oriented governments came to power in Somalia and Ethiopia. Russian interests, on the other hand, can be traced back to the eighteenth century.[1] The Soviet Union established a diplomatic mission in Addis Ababa in 1943, and the first Soviet ambassador took up his post in May 1956.[2] In 1959 Haile Selassie became the first ever African head of state to pay an official visit to the Soviet Union, an event which – in the year of the Cuban revolution – highlights, even under Khrushchev, Moscow's non-ideological, opportunistic foreign policy. Later the Soviet Union was to provide neighbouring Somalia, which had recently been granted independence, with a military-aid programme worth $30 million. However, the border dispute which was eventually to lead to war was already a contentious issue between Mogadishu and Addis Ababa. Khrushchev states in his memoirs that the USSR had 'excellent relations' with Haile Selassie, and thus 'we were in a rather delicate situation and had to exercise a certain amount of diplomatic flexibility'.[3] The Soviet leader sent Ya. A. Malik, the Deputy Foreign Minister, to Addis Ababa in March 1964 to reassure the Ethiopians that the military assistance to Somalia would not be used against the Ogaden.[4]

Moscow's interests in the Horn are essentially strategic, for it is situated between two continents and is close to a vital sea passage linking European Russia with the Soviet Far East. The Soviet Union had sought to gain a strategic foothold in the region since the 1950s, but, despite showing a good deal of 'diplomatic flexibility' in relations with Egypt and the Sudan, it did not appear to achieve a real breakthrough until the 1970s, when two radical governments came to power that both advocated a socialist path of development.

The problem, though, was the unresolved border dispute between them, and when this eventually came to a head in 1977, the Soviet Union was forced to take sides.

In contrast, Cuba in the 1960s did not seek to play an active role in the Horn of Africa. It was even slow to establish diplomatic relations with the Supreme Revolutionary Council which had taken power in Somalia in October 1969, despite its publicly proclaimed commitment to a socialist path of development. This initial reluctance to identify with the new regime in Mogadishu could have been due to a suspicion that a coup carried out by professional military officers – as opposed to a revolution of national liberation carried out by a guerrilla army, as in Algeria – would be unable to break out of the imperialist embrace.

However, in the late 1960s and early 1970s, a number of events led to a re-evaluation of Cuban attitudes and strategies towards several states that were following a path in their foreign policies that was independent of that of the United States. In 1968 a progressive military regime in Peru began nationalizing US multinational corporations; Bolivia nationalized the US Gulf Oil Corporation the following year; in 1970 Chile elected a socialist government; and Jamaica did the same in 1972. Cuba now initiated a policy of establishing diplomatic relations with any state that it considered to be acting independently of the United States.

The establishment of diplomatic relations with Somalia in July 1972 (the same month that Cuba established relations with Peru) should be seen in the context of Castro's new commitment to diplomacy, and not necessarily as a total identification with the goals of the Revolutionary Council in Mogadishu. Nevertheless, it is apparent that Cuba had now come to accept that there were different paths to socialism – something which the Soviet leadership had acknowledged soon after Stalin's death. In the 1960s the Cubans had publicly condemned peaceful coexistence as a sell-out to the imperialists, but in July 1972 Castro gave a speech in Moscow in which he expressed Cuban support for Brezhnev's policy of detente.[5] However, he made it clear that his support for detente would not undermine his commitment to the ideological struggle or to national liberation movements. Events in Angola just a couple of years later bore this out.

In the Horn of Africa, Cuba's commitment to internationalist socialist solidarity and the ideological struggle is much more questionable. The first joint communiqué signed by Cuba and Somalia, just three weeks after relations had been established, acknowledged the right of the indigenous Somalis in the Ogaden region to 'reunification' with their ethnic relatives across the border.[6] By signing this communiqué, Cuba was in effect accepting the rights of the Somali population in neighbouring Ethiopia, Kenya and Djibouti to self-determination, provided that this was achieved through peaceful means. Castro was in a difficult position if he was to be consistent with his ideological beliefs, for the Somalis of the Ogaden were theoretically no less the victims of colonization than were the Angolans, Mozambicans, Zimbabweans and the people of Namibia; the only difference was that the colonizers in the Ogaden were not white Europeans. However, whereas in the other cases the Organization of African Unity (OAU) supported the rights of these peoples to self-determination, the position of the Somalis in the Ogaden was deemed to have been settled when the European colonizers left the Horn. Castro accepted the OAU ruling while nevertheless giving, at least initially, verbal support to Somalia's claims. As Nelson P. Valdes puts it, Cuba 'wanted to broaden its diplomatic ties, while remaining true to Marxist principles on the nationalities question and avoiding any breach of international law'.[7] There was no such contradiction in the attitude of the Soviet Union, which accepted the OAU ruling without reservation.

In June 1974 Cuba signed a technical and cultural agreement with Somalia, and the following month President Podgorny signed a twenty-year Treaty of Friendship and Cooperation in Mogadishu. In other words, both Cuba and the Soviet Union were making deeper commitments to the Somali regime just as the Selassie dictatorship in neighbouring Ethiopia was about to collapse. The Ethiopian dictator was overthrown in a military coup in September 1974, and the Provisional Military Council (PMAC) that seized power became increasingly radicalized until, by February 1977, after internal struggles, Mengistu Haile-Mariam headed the Council and deliberately began to steer Ethiopia along a socialist path of development. Cuba had established diplomatic relations with the PMAC in July 1975, but close bilateral ties did not develop until Mengistu had consolidated his leadership. Up until February 1977 Cuba focused its attention on Somalia, limiting its involvement with Ethiopia to low-level diplomatic contacts. However, Cuba was the first government to send a telegram of congratulation to Mengistu, and *Granma* printed on its front page the next day a feature praising the victory of the 'radical wing' of the PMAC.[8] Moscow and Havana viewed the developments in the Horn of Africa in a most positive light, since both Somalia and Ethiopia were moving away from the imperialist camp and taking steps to construct socialism. However, the similarity in ideological beliefs of the two African states was not enough to prevent hostility from breaking out over a territorial dispute.

The coordination of Soviet and Cuban policies towards Ethiopia, in contrast to Angola, can be deduced by examining the high-level political and military contacts between the two sides at critical points in the decision-making process. When the Ethiopians dispatched a secret mission to Moscow in 1975 with a request for military equipment, Grechko, Kosygin and other Soviet officials made it plain that they would only provide the PMAC with arms if the pro-Western elements in the Council were purged and the Soviet Union could be assured that the arms would not be used to intimidate Somalia (and hence undermine Soviet relations with Mogadishu).[9] The Ethiopians left Moscow empty-handed. Meanwhile, the deteriorating situation, aggravated by Soviet supplies of arms to Somalia during the early 1970s, was sliding towards a major confrontation between the two African states in the Ogaden. Under Selassie, Ethiopia had relied upon US military aid; now, because its radicalized revolution was moving towards a civil war, President Carter was reluctant to keep the PMAC supplied with arms. The Ethiopians turned again to the Soviet Union in December 1976, by which time the pro-Western elements were being removed from the Council. On this occasion a secret arms deal was signed. At the same time as this agreement was being worked out in Moscow, Raúl Castro and Rafael Rodríguez were also in the Soviet capital, where they held talks with Brezhnev on international issues.[10] Just a few days earlier General Viktor Kulikov, the Soviet First Deputy Minister of Defence, had been in Havana.[11] The Soviet Union and Cuba, acting in coordination with one another, were seeking to take advantage of the developing situation in the Horn. The prospects for establishing two friendly socialist regimes appeared to be favourable, but war between the two states over the Ogaden had to be prevented if such an outcome were to be assured.

Both Fidel Castro and Nikolai Podgorny, the Soviet President, embarked upon separate, but probably previously coordinated, diplomatic missions to Africa in March 1977 in an attempt at crisis prevention. Castro visited a number of African and Arab countries (Algeria, Angola, Libya, Mozambique, Somalia, Tanzania and South Yemen), before going on to Moscow to confer with the Soviet leadership.[12] While in Yemen Castro arranged a meeting between Siad Barre, the Somali leader, and Mengistu, in which he proposed the establishment of a political federation of socialist-oriented states incorporating South Yemen, Ethiopia, Eritrea, Somalia, and Djibouti. Castro stated one year later that his diplomatic mission, which marked Cuba's first active involvement in the Horn, was undertaken in order to 'avoid a betrayal of the international revolutionary movement' and 'to prevent the leadership of Somalia, with its territorial ambitions and aggressive attitude, from going over to imperialism'.[13] Immediately on the heels of Castro, Podgorny paid a visit to Mogadishu to bolster this joint Soviet-Cuban initiative, and then the two men met in Moscow a few days later to discuss the matter with Brezhnev, Kosygin and Gromyko.[14] The joint mission failed to resolve the dispute between the two African states, and Soviet arms shipments began to arrive in Ethiopia at about the same time as the first contingent of Cuban military advisers.

Ethiopia had cut off its ties with the United States in April 1977, and the following month Mengistu was in Moscow, where he signed a second agreement for the supply of Soviet arms. It was one of the largest arms agreements the Soviet Union had ever signed with a Third World country, and was estimated to be worth between $350 million and $450 million.[15] During the summer the dual threat to Mengistu – from the Eritreans in the north and the Somalis in the south – increased in intensity and, despite their wish to avoid a final confrontation in the Horn, Moscow and Havana were placed in a position of having to take sides. In the United States the Carter administration hinted that it might provide arms to Somalia, and in Britain the Foreign and Commonwealth Office announced that it intended to do so.[16] Encouraged by these announcements, the Somali army invaded the Ogaden province of Ethiopia in July. That same month the Soviet Defence Minister, Ustinov, invited Raúl Castro, the Cuban Minister of the Revolutionary Armed Forces, to Moscow for an unscheduled meeting.[17] It is very likely that the sudden meeting was arranged to discuss the situation in the Horn and to coordinate Soviet and Cuban military strategy. Further evidence of the high level of coordination within the socialist bloc is provided by Raúl Castro's stop-over, on his way back to Havana, in East Berlin, where he held talks with General Heinz Hoffmann, East Germany's Minister of Defence.[18] An unknown number of East German military advisers also participated in the war in the Horn, alongside the Cuban and Soviet contingents.[19]

Siad Barre was in Moscow in August in a last-ditch attempt to persuade Moscow not to back the Ethiopian government in the conflict, but his protestations to Kosygin, Gromyko and Suslov came to nothing; the Soviet Union stopped all military deliveries to Mogadishu.[20] Meanwhile, the Soviet Union and Cuba were engaged in a tightly coordinated strategy of military cooperation with the Ethiopian regime. In mid-September a Soviet military delegation arrived in the Ethiopian capital; in October the Ethiopian Foreign Minister paid a visit to Havana; and later that month Mengistu himself held talks with Fidel Castro in the Cuban capital. In early November Raúl paid another visit to Moscow, accompanied on this occasion by some Cuban generals who later played a leading role in the Ogaden war. A high-level Ethiopian delegation was also in Moscow at this time; so trilateral negotiations could have taken place to discuss the planning of the Soviet-Cuban military intervention. Just one week after these events in Moscow Somalia cut off diplomatic relations with Cuba, expelled all Soviet advisers from the country and unilaterally renounced the 1974 Treaty of Friendship and Cooperation.[21] This was the final signal for Moscow and Havana to put into action the strategy of cooperative intervention that they had been planning.

The evidence, I believe, strongly indicates that the conception and planning of the cooperative intervention strategy was a direct result of joint consultations between Soviet and Cuban political and military leaders. Evidence that the actual implementation of the strategy was tightly coordinated is perhaps even stronger. Cuban troops and Soviet advisers and arms began arriving in Ethiopia in late October. Whereas, in the case of Angola, Cuban troops had initially been dispatched under their own steam following an independent decision to send them, the Cuban troops that were sent to Ethiopia travelled in Soviet transport aircraft via Moscow, and the decision to send them was made jointly. The operation itself was coordinated by high-level officials from both the Soviet Union and Cuba. Raúl Castro flew secretly to Addis Ababa in January 1978, travelling on from there to Moscow as part of the coordinated strategy. General Vasili Petrov, First Deputy Commander of the Soviet ground forces, and other Soviet officers were in Ethiopia overseeing the actual military operations conducted by Ethiopian and Cuban troops.[22] The Cuban intervention in the war in the Horn proved, as in Angola, to be decisive to the outcome. By March 1978 some 12,000 or more Cuban troops had helped to push the Somali army out of the Ogaden and back across the border into Somalia.

Cuba's decision to assist Ethiopia in its struggle to regain the Ogaden from Somalia led to a re-evaluation of the idea of national liberation for the Somalis in the region. Earlier Cuba had given verbal support to the idea of national self-determination for all ethnic Somalis in a Greater Somalia; now, even if pursued through peaceful means, such a concept was unacceptable to the Cubans. Castro instead maintained that Somalia had no historical claims to the Ogaden, and that sowing divisions between races within the existing African boundaries could only serve the interests of the West in its attempts to weaken the 'revolutionary forces'.[23] The Cuban leader had come to accept the OAU ruling on the territorial integrity of the state system in decolonized Africa, and, when Mengistu paid a visit to Havana in April 1978, a joint Cuban-Ethiopian communiqué was issued in which Somalia was called upon to renounce its 'expansionist designs' on Ethiopia, Kenya and Djibouti.[24] Given the geopolitical and ethnic realities of the situation in Africa, this was the most practical line to take – but it did contradict earlier Cuban pronouncements on the issue.

As Robbins notes, 'It is a basic tenet of Cuban ideology that internationalist responsibilities take precedence over narrower state interests or bloc commitments.'[25] In the Horn of Africa, Cuba was faced with a dilemma: two socialist states were about to go to war with one another over a territorial issue relating to what in essence was historically an unresolved colonial question. In the event Castro sided with Ethiopia because of Somalia's violation of the principles of non-intervention and territorial integrity. Interestingly, he justified this decision in *realpolitik* terms. In March 1978 he explicitly acknowledged the inviolability of the state boundaries in Africa left by colonialism, and, when justifying Cuban participation in the war, he spoke not only of the intrigues of 'imperialism' but also of the strategic importance of the Horn for NATO in its calculations of the balance of power.[26]

Nearly twenty years after the Cuban revolution, was Castro perhaps becoming less of an ideologue and more of a realist? This question takes on added significance in the light of Cuban attitudes and policies towards the Eritrean issue. Here Soviet and Cuban perceptions and strategies differ, yet despite the asymmetry in economic and military power between the two states, the Soviet Union was unable, if indeed it tried, to influence Cuba to take an active combat role against the Eritreans. Nevertheless, Cuba's military mission in the Ogaden had the effect of allowing regular Ethiopian troops to redeploy to the north in order to take up the fight against the Eritreans, who were fighting for self-determination. Thus indirectly Cuba was, and still is in 1987, assisting the Ethiopians in their military struggle against Eritrea.

Eritrea's history is complex. A mixture of several ethnic groups, it has been colonized by various neighbouring and distant states during the past two centuries. Egypt exercised sovereignty over Eritrea until the Italians colonized the area in 1886. The British seized Eritrea in 1941 and maintained a colonial trusteeship there until 1950, when the United Nations established it as an autonomous region in federation with Ethiopia. Then, against the wishes of the Eritreans, who advocated independence, Haile Selassie unilaterally annexed Eritrea as a province of Ethiopia in 1962.[27] The Cubans viewed Eritrea as a colony of Ethiopia and supported the Eritreans in their struggle for independence at least up until the overthrow of Selassie, possibly beyond. However, following a period of silence on the issue as the Castro government was assessing its new relationship with the radical military regime in Addis Ababa, the Cubans publicly withdrew their support for the Eritreans in February 1977, arguing now that they were a tool of US imperialism.

Yet the status of Eritrea had not changed, nor had the Marxist credentials of those fighting for liberation. This about-turn was very difficult to square with Cuba's previous revolutionary commitment to national liberation, and one has to ask whether the Soviet Union played a part in influencing this switch in policy. For here we do have a concrete case in which Cuba changed its behaviour, and, more significantly perhaps, this change in behaviour assisted the Soviet Union in its geostrategic priorities while undermining the credibility of Cuba's ideological commitment to Third World national liberation. However, despite the observable change in

Cuban behaviour (cutting off aid to the Eritreans), there are no written sources to confirm or refute the proposition that the Soviet Union offered carrots or wielded a stick. It should also be noted that the USSR changed its behaviour. It, too, had supported the Eritreans before the overthrow of Selassie, but then this was in keeping with traditional Soviet pragmatism. Furthermore, although the Cubans did stop supporting the Eritreans, they did not actively support the Ethiopian government by sending combat troops to the northern front.

Cuba was in fact placed in a dilemma, as it had been over the Ogaden war. For the Soviet Union, there was no such dilemma: Eritrea provided alternative bases and outlets to the sea to those that had been lost in Somalia following the severance of relations. Without Eritrea Ethiopia would be a land-locked country, and hence of much less strategic value to the Soviet Union. (The Eritrean port at Massawa controls the waterway connecting the Gulf of Aden to the Red Sea.) The Soviet Union's superpower interests in its global competition with the United States led to what was viewed in Moscow as a rational choice to support Mengistu in his struggle against the Eritreans. Cuba, on the other hand, with its primary interest in the North-South 'struggle', and Castro's personal foreign-policy goal of leading the Third World in this struggle, did not have a clear choice among the alternatives. If Castro had pulled his troops out of Ethiopia, the Mengistu regime's security would have been weakened, and socialist development threatened. If he had sent Cuban troops to the Eritrean front, he would have been actively supporting the colonization and subjugation of a Marxist liberation movement, and thus threatening Cuba's image in the Third World. In the event he chose to do neither of these things, and left Cuban combat troops in place in the south of Ethiopia to defend against any further aggression from Somalia. This way Castro hoped to ensure the continuance of Mengistu's regime (by freeing Ethiopian troops in the Ogaden to fight in the north) while at the same time not tarnishing his image in the Non-Aligned Movement (by ensuring Cuban combat troops did not take up direct battle with the Eritreans).

The only other alternative would have been to resupply the Eritreans with arms, a course more in keeping with Cuban ideology. But one should not overestimate the role of ideology in the formulation of any nation-state's foreign policy, even Cuba's. I have noted that ideological commitment has been more important in Cuban than in Soviet foreign policy from the 1960s through to the war in Angola. The same is probably true today. It is also an empirical fact that all revolutionary states which begin their existence challenging the status quo, and the norms and customs of international behaviour, come ultimately to accept them and to act, out of enlightened self-interest, in accordance with them. Ideology is not always a neat and logical guide for policy formulation, and in this particular case Castro was confronted with a problem which had no simple solution.

It has often been suggested that the Soviet Union asked for Cuban troops to be used in the struggle against the Eritreans, but that Castro refused.[28] There is no evidence to verify this claim, although it is true that the Soviet Union has been much less publicly committed than the Cubans to a peaceful solution to the conflict. The Ethiopian government itself has shown no real commitment to diplomacy, relying entirely on military force. Castro has called for a just political solution and stated on a number of occasions that this should be brought about on the basis of a 'Marxist-Leninist' approach to the problem.[29] Raymond Duncan even goes so far as to suggest that Cuba has influenced Moscow on this issue, by encouraging the Soviet Union to give more backing to a negotiated solution and by weakening its commitment to the military option.[30] Once more, however, we do not have any evidence to show definitively who influenced whom over Eritrea. By examining only bilateral Soviet-Cuban relations, we may be ignoring other important intervening factors. For example, Castro may have been more influenced by Iraq, Mozambique, Algeria, the Malagasy Republic and other Third World states which we know communicated a desire that he desist from sending Cubans into combat against the Eritreans. His policy may also have been affected by pressures from other, less friendly states that threatened not only his leading position in the Non-Aligned Movement, but even his membership of it.[31]

In summary, a number of points should be made. First, the Soviet Union and Cuba acted in tight coordination in developing a joint policy and strategy in the Horn of Africa from the very outset. Second, as the situation in the Horn deteriorated, both Moscow and Havana kept in regular contact in order to adjust the strategy accordingly. Third, there was close coordination in actually implementing the strategy, since the initial diplomatic effort and the eventual military intervention both involved joint participation. In other words, in direct contrast to Angola, the Soviet Union and Cuba acted in concert. In an interview with a former senior member of the Cuban Foreign Ministry who specialized in African affairs at this time, I was told of the great geostrategic importance of Eritrea and of the need, for this reason, to maintain Ethiopia's sovereignty over the province. 'No one,' he stated, 'commits suicide for a just cause.'[32] Castro's Cuba had initially embarked upon a far-reaching global foreign policy out of ideological commitment, but now ideology as a motivating factor was being tempered by realism. Cuba and the Soviet Union reached the same foreign-policy positions in the Ogaden and Eritrea through a joint decision-making process, and although their objectives were not in either case identical, there was some convergence of interests in the Horn of Africa.

7

CENTRAL AMERICA AND THE CARIBBEAN

Changing world views
Cuba is a Latin American country, and Latin America has always been a central concern of its foreign policy. The Soviet Union is a Eurasian superpower with weak historical, ideological, political and economic links with Latin America, which, in addition, is strategically far less important in Moscow's security calculations than almost any other region in the world. Until the early 1960s the Soviet Union paid scant attention to the area, but the Cuban revolution led to a re-evaluation of Soviet thinking and to a plethora of scholarly writings on the revolutionary potential of Latin American states. Yet in the 1960s Moscow and Havana disagreed fundamentally about the lessons and significance that the Cuban revolutionary experience had for other countries in Latin America. Castro considered that the success of the 26 July Movement in Cuba proved conclusively that the only road to revolution was a military one and the only tool for achieving it was a small guerrilla army. The Soviet Union, on the other hand, argued that the proper revolutionary model depended on the objective circumstances in a particular state, and that in most Latin American states circumstances dictated a peaceful road to revolution.

Cuba eventually terminated its active support for other Latin American guerrilla movements and ceased publicly propagating its militant revolutionary doctrine. This was in part due to Soviet influence, and in part to the simple fact that US-trained counter-insurgency forces had all but completely destroyed the military challenges to the Latin American governments. Che Guevara's death in Bolivia in 1967 symbolized the failure of Cuba's revolutionary strategy, and the democratic election of Salvador Allende in Chile three years later vindicated the Soviet model of peaceful change – or so it seemed to many at the time. Allende headed a five-party coalition which included the pro-Soviet Communist Party, and one of his first acts was to re-establish diplomatic relations with Cuba, just one week after taking office (the Soviet Union had had unbroken relations with Chile since November 1964).[1]

The Soviet Union clearly viewed Allende's victory in a very positive light. A large number of articles by leading scholars and statesmen were published which argued that the peaceful road to socialism, led by the vanguard parties of the working class, had been justified by the events in Chile.[2] General-Secretary Brezhnev referred to Allende's victory as the 'most important recent event in Latin America'.[3] Castro, too, approved of the new radical government in Chile, but his enthusiasm was restrained by doubts about the viability of the 'peaceful revolution'. He expressed these fears in November 1971, one year after Allende had taken power, in a speech at Santiago's National Stadium during an official state visit to Chile. The Cuban leader spoke of his 'curiosity' and 'interest' in the revolutionary process in Chile which 'is unique in the history of humanity trying to carry out a revolutionary process by legal and constitutional methods, using the very laws ... that the exploiters created to maintain their class domination'.[4] He spoke of his 'solidarity' and 'moral support' for the Chilean revolution, but warned that resistance to it would grow among the 'exploiting classes', for never in history had the privileged members of the ruling classes resigned themselves to peaceful change.

It was plain that Castro had grave reservations from the outset about the success of the peaceful road to socialism, although he was deliberately careful in his statements not to 'create more difficulties for Allende's government'.[5] However, he did state, in a question-and-answer session with students at the University of Concepcion, that 'the theses of Che continue in full force'.[6] Later, in a press conference in Santiago, Castro acknowledged that he had little faith in the electoral process, since when it did bring a socialist government to power, imperialists and the privileged classes would seek to overthrow it. Therefore, 'if the oppressors and the privileged block all roads, there'll be no other way open for the peoples but that of revolutionary violence'.[7] At the press conference Castro refused to answer a question on what he thought about the Chilean armed forces, although he had stated a couple of days earlier that he had spoken at length with members of the Chilean military, and of all the groups he had met the military and the church 'were the source of the greatest irritation'.[8]

It is clear, then, that the Soviet Union and Cuba, even at this more stable stage of their relationship, still had serious differences of opinion regarding the proper path to socialist revolution. As it turned out Castro's fears were justified, for less than two years later, in September 1973, Allende was murdered in a coup which brought the military to power. Cuba declared an official three-day period of mourning and the Cuban press, which gave the coup massive coverage, stated without reservation that 'armed struggle' was now the *only* way for revolution in Chile.[9] The Soviet Union cut off diplomatic relations with the Pinochet regime on 22 September 1973, but otherwise its reaction was far more restrained than Cuba's.[10] Again, these different responses to the events in Chile reflect the different political priorities of the two countries rather than strict differences in ideology – even if these too were important. Since the early 1970s Castro had been stressing the common interests of the Latin American states and the need for Latin American solidarity in pressing for a more just and equitable world economic order. The Soviet Union's principal foreign-policy objective was to improve relations with the United States, since this was the basis for achieving its other goals. Brezhnev did not want to sacrifice superpower detente to developments in a country of no strategic or economic significance.

Yet the events in Chile did provide a lesson for Soviet scholars in their assessment of the revolutionary potential of Latin American states. What is interesting here is that eventually most of them came to accept the Cuban theory of revolution. The one issue over which Moscow and Havana had almost ruptured their relations, and which had led to the one clear instance of Soviet influence being asserted, was now finally resolved, with the Soviet position moving in line with Cuba's. This is not to suggest that Cuba influenced Soviet perceptions, although this is almost certainly true to an extent, but rather that the Soviet Union changed its perceptions according to changing circumstances. Likewise, the Soviet Union did not now consider it appropriate to 'export' revolution; it had not changed its attitude on this matter. Nor did it advocate armed struggle as the *only* means of revolution. This still depended on the 'objective' circumstances in a particular state.

An analysis of the writings of Soviet scholars in the research institutes and of leading figures in the International Department of the CPSU Central Committee after the Chilean experience and up to the victory of the Sandinistas in Nicaragua shows how Soviet views changed. The first interpretation of the coup against Allende was given by Boris Ponomarev, head of the International Department. Ponomarev did not rule out the peaceful path to socialism, but he did refer to the necessity of gaining control of the professional military and to the need to employ extraparliamentary means to ensure the survival of the revolution.[11] Sergei Mikoyan, son of the late Politburo member Anastas Mikoyan and editor of the Latin American Insitute's journal, *Latinskaia Amerika*, similarly did not rule out a non-violent path, yet also stressed that in future it would be necessary to ensure control over the military.[12] An examination of other writings indicates that one important lesson gained from the Chilean experience was that in order to succeed, a revolution must be able to defend itself.[13] Another lesson was that a revolution must have the full support of the masses, not only the urban working class but also other groups such as the peasantry, the progressive members of the bourgeoisie and the Church.[14] The communist party was still judged to be the natural revolutionary vanguard, but more attention was paid in the scholarly literature to the possibility of a revolutionary army overthrowing the established order; the party could play a less important role in the initial stages of the revolution.[15] Finally, once in power, the revolutionary authorities should immediately nationalize the 'commanding heights' of industry, but proceed at a slower pace with other areas of the economy, so as not to alienate the bourgeoisie, a strategy resembling the New Economic Policy (NEP) during the 1920s in the Soviet Union.[16]

Thus, by the time of the Sandinista victory in 1979, Soviet and Cuban views of the appropriate revolutionary path and post-revolutionary strategy were converging. Both sides now argued that military struggle conducted by a guerrilla army with the support of large sections of the population could gain power and avoid the mistakes made in Chile in the early 1970s. Events in Central America

– and, indeed, Cuba's own experience – seemed to verify the utility of this revolutionary model. By 1979 Cuba and the Soviet Union had come to a similar view of developments in Latin America and had reached a compromise on the conduct of their foreign policies. Wherever a revolution appeared to be a feasible proposition, both sides would give it their support. Where there was little prospect for a successful revolution, the two states would seek to maintain links with the existing governments.[17]

The Soviet change in perceptions and policies was due more to experience than to any direct influence from Cuba. However, the Cuban revolution itself had had an impact, and it is not unreasonable to assume that Soviet party officials, officials from the foreign and trade ministries, scholars, and military personnel who had had direct contact with their Cuban counterparts had learned from their personal experience. In this sense Cubans surely did have an influence on the changing Soviet view. After all, Cuba is a Caribbean country with a much better understanding of the region and far better contacts with revolutionary movements than the Soviet Union. Furthermore, despite their convergence of views, the Soviet Union and Cuba reacted differently to some events in Grenada and Nicaragua during the period 1979–86, and what evidence is available suggests that Cuban influence made the Soviet Union change its policy, rather than the other way around. In order to illustrate this, I shall examine Soviet and Cuban reactions and policies towards the New Jewel Movement and the Sandinista revolution.

Grenada

When US marines landed on the Caribbean island of Grenada in October 1983, they did not discover well-armed regular troops of the Cuban Revolutionary Armed Forces (although they met some resistance from Cuban construction workers). They did find some 11,000 internal documents of the New Jewel Movement (NJM) and a number of secret bilateral treaties concluded with the Soviet Union. In a foreword to a selection of these documents which has since been published, it is claimed that they reveal Grenada 'was being readied as a pawn, like Cuba before it, in the struggle for world hegemony'.[18] President Reagan argued soon after the invasion that Grenada was being converted into a 'Soviet-Cuban colony' from which revolution was to be exported throughout the Caribbean; hence the marines had arrived in the 'nick of time'.[19] Such assumptions about the Soviet-Cuban link in revolutionary Grenada in the early 1980s are common, among US politicians and scholars.[20] The basic logic of their arguments leads to the conclusion that Cuba, at the behest of the Soviet Union, was helping to create another Marxist-Leninist state which would then, like Cuba, further Soviet expansionist designs in America's 'strategic rear'. Yet a careful reading of the Grenadian documents produces a very different conclusion.

It should be stressed at the outset that in analysing these documents (I use here those released by the US Departments of State and Defense in 1984),[21] one has to bear in mind who is saying what to whom and under what circumstances. The documents discovered are all Grenadian internal ones in the English language, and *not* Soviet or Cuban internal documents in the Russian or Spanish languages, although the secret military treaties are in both English and Russian. Thus we have to be careful in deducing Soviet or Cuban goals from sources which, for the most part, are concered with domestic Grenadian issues. These documents provide a clear insight into the internal wranglings of the NJM, and they also give important clues to Soviet and Cuban attitudes and policies.

If anything the documents reveal a strong reluctance on the part of the Soviet Union to commit itself to the New Jewel Movement's revolution (significantly referred to in Moscow as a *coup d'état* (*gosudarstvennyi povorot*)).[22] Castro was one of the first foreign leaders to applaud the NJM's seizure of power from Sir Eric Gairy in March 1979, and within a month Cuba had established diplomatic relations with the new People's Revolutionary Government (PRG) in St George's, headed by Maurice Bishop.[23] The Soviet Union did not establish diplomatic relations with the NJM until six months later, and then the negotiations were conducted through Cuban channels, and the formal communiqué was signed in Havana, not Moscow or St Georges.[24] This was the first indication of the important role Cuba was playing in influencing the Soviet leadership in its relations with the NJM. Indeed, as Richard Jacobs, the Grenadian ambassador in Moscow, put it, if Cuba had not 'championed our cause', the Soviet Union would have been unwilling to commit itself to Grenada.[25]

Richard Jacobs had earlier served as ambassador in Havana, and through the Cubans he would have gained some good contacts for his later posting to Moscow. However, as his dispatches from the Soviet Union clearly show, the Soviet leaders were extremely cautious in forging close ties to Grenada. Jacobs himself, in a personal letter to the PRG in July 1983, stated that the reason for Soviet caution was that Grenada figured only 'in a very minute way in the USSR's global relationships'.[26] One of his deputies in the Moscow embassy also wrote a letter to Bishop pointing out that the Russians were very sceptical in their dealings with the NJM.[27] In his own dispatch, Jacobs referred to the Soviet Union's refusal either to meet diplomatically at the highest levels or to show reciprocity in diplomatic protocol – a source of constant irritation and frustration to the status-conscious NJM. This refusal to deal at the highest levels of party and government stood in direct contrast to the relations being developed between Nicaragua and the Soviet Union. Whereas Bishop's requests to meet with Brezhnev and, following his death, Andropov, were politely turned down, Daniel Ortega of the Sandinistas was given an audience with both General-Secretaries. Nicaragua, because of its size, population and strategic position, was far more important to the Soviet Union than a tiny spice island with little relevance to the overall correlation of forces.

The Soviet Union did sign a number of bilateral trade agreements with the Grenadian government, the first of which, in June 1980, committed both sides to purchasing certain products at 'standard world market prices'.[28] However, it provided only very small amounts of developmental aid to the NJM: a limited number of scholarships, the delivery of a handful of cars and buses, and assistance in the construction of a new party headquarters. The single most important project in Grenada, the construction of a new airport for boosting the tourist industry, received no Soviet financial support at all. Prime Minister Bishop met with Foreign Minister Gromyko in Moscow in April 1983 and appealed for a Soviet grant of $6 million. He was turned down. The NJM also hoped that the Soviet Union would purchase 1,000 tons of nutmeg, but was informed that the USSR would only import what it consumed each year (200–300 tons), and then only at 'the world market price or below'.[29]

It is true that the Soviet Union was far more generous with military aid, and it is this fact that has led many to the conclusion that Moscow's intention was to construct a military bastion from which to export revolution throughout the Caribbean. Significantly, two of the three secret agreements to supply the People's Revolutionary Army (PRA) with military equipment were concluded in Havana, thereby underlining the role the Cubans played on behalf of Bishop's government. The top secret agreements make it clear that Moscow was prepared to supply and deliver, via Cuba, some 20 million roubles' worth of military hardware, free of charge, over the course of three years between 1980 and 1983.[30] However, there is absolutely no indication in the documents that the military equipment was designed for any other purpose than to defend Grenada itself. Members of the NJM, as the recorded minutes of its Politburo and Central Committee adequately demonstrate, were seriously, and in the event justifiably, concerned about the possibility of external aggression. Furthermore, the lesson of Chile in 1973, which has constantly been repeated in Soviet writings, is that a revolution must be able to defend itself. The Soviet Union was supplying the PRG with the military hardware necessary (but ultimately insufficient) for this task.

The Soviet Union's commitment to Grenada was minimal; its assistance was limited and only provided as a result of Cuban lobbying on behalf of the Bishop regime. A former official of the Cuban Foreign Ministry with responsibility for the Caribbean stated that the Cubans had to persuade Moscow of the political importance of Grenada. This, apparently, took some time, for initially the Soviet Union considered developments in Grenada to be totally irrelevant to its own foreign-policy objectives.[31] By contrast, Cuba, a Caribbean country itself, accorded Grenada far more importance from the outset. Whereas the Soviet leadership would not give an audience to Bishop, Fidel Castro fostered a very close personal friendship with the Grenadian leader. Their revolutionary experiences were very different, but the two men had much in common in terms of their style of leadership and identification with the Third World.

Castro's commitment to the Grenadian revolution was absolute. He considered it part of his internationalist duty to provide as much assistance as his country could reasonably offer, and the strongest reflection of Cuba's solidarity was the fraternal aid given to help construct the airport at Point Salines. Within the first four weeks of seizing power, the NJM had received from Cuba a substantial quantity of small arms and military advisers to train the PRA in their use.[32] This was at a time when the Brezhnev leadership in

Moscow was still deciding on its response to the new situation in Grenada. In a speech to the Second Congress of the Cuban Communist Party, Bishop thanked Castro for his support and acknowledged the influence of the Cuban revolutionary experience on the NJM: 'Cuba has been a beacon for us in Grenada. It has both taught and reminded us of many important lessons.'[33] A report from Grenada's embassy in Havana listed 22 different areas of collaboration that had developed between the two countries by 1980.[34]

It can be confidently stated from the evidence available that in this instance Cuba influenced the Soviet Union and made it change its behaviour. The Soviet leadership under Brezhnev had become far more cautious in committing resources to poor Third World states, particularly in the case of Grenada, a distant island of little economic, political or strategic importance. For Cuba, though, Grenada was a neighbouring island which held out the promise of increasing Cuba's prestige and further undermining the power of the United States. In so far as the Soviet Union did finally give some aid to Grenada, Cuba achieved its objective, not by threats or promises (at least as far as we know), but by insistent and prolonged persuasion. The most interesting aspect of the whole affair, however, is the question of Soviet and Cuban behaviour over the internal NJM split between Maurice Bishop and Bernard Coard, which finally resulted in the US-led invasion.

Circumstantial evidence indicates that the Soviet Union and Cuba supported different sides in the internal party struggle within the leading ranks of the NJM, with Moscow supporting Coard and Havana supporting Bishop. Bishop was the more charismatic leader and tended to make decisions outside the confines of the NJM's party apparatus. Coard, on the other hand, advocated a strict adherence to the principles of democratic centralism within a monolithic Marxist-Leninist party structure. Bishop was much more the pragmatist, Coard the dogmatist. Coard's faction within the NJM had closer ties with the Soviet Union, in terms of contacts with Soviet officials and numbers of visits to Moscow; the supporters of Bishop had closer ties with Cuba.[35]

In a major speech after the invasion of Grenada Castro compared Coard to Pol Pot and made it clear whom he supported in the intra-party struggle for power: 'This group of Coard's that seized power in Grenada expressed serious reservations regarding Cuba from the very beginning because of our well-known and unquestionable friendship with Bishop.'[36] In contrast, the Soviet Union's initial reaction to the invasion was restricted to a criticism of the USA's interference in the internal affairs of a sovereign state; there was no blame or condemnation of Coard for provoking the crisis.[37] A few months later, however, the Soviet Union did publish a special volume on Grenada in which Coard's faction of the Central Committee was said to have been infiltrated by CIA agents.[38] Nevertheless, it is unclear how far Moscow and Havana had a conflict of interests in Grenada; the meetings of the NJM Central Committee that were called to resolve the leadership issue show clearly that the Soviet Union and Cuba and their relations with Grenada were not on the agenda at all.[39]

Yet the Cubans may have been preparing to intervene on behalf of Bishop. According to Lynden Rhamdany, former Grenadian Minister of Tourism, the Cuban ambassador in St George's had managed to contact Bishop twice just before his murder, offering to help. Bishop turned him down. Further evidence is to be found in a letter from a Cuban soldier to his family in which he states that, 'On the 19th I was selected to go on a rescue mission of Bishop but when we were prepared the news arrived that they had shot him along with his companions.'[40] A Cuban official who knew personally the two actors in the power struggle in Grenada stated that the Cubans supported Bishop because he 'had more sense of reality', whereas Coard was 'too disciplined a theoretician' and too rigidly ideological in his orientation.[41] An eminent Soviet scholar, on the other hand, suggests that the leaders in Moscow were concerned about the prospect of Bishop turning into another Tito (who was interestingly compared to Castro).[42] It is most likely that there was indeed a strong difference of opinion in Havana and Moscow over the leadership issue in Grenada, but Castro, undaunted by Soviet power, continued to conduct an independent policy, even possibly to the point of considering intervening on the side least favoured in the Kremlin.

In summary it can be argued that, in the case of Grenada, Cuba conducted an independent policy that was strongly supportive of Bishop and the NJM, whereas Moscow did not even have a policy towards the island during the first few months after Gairy's ouster. Cuba then spent a considerable amount of time and effort trying to convince the Soviet Union of the importance of the Grenadian revolution as a political example to other states in the Caribbean. Cuban lobbying worked, although the Soviet commitment never completely satisfied the demands of the NJM, as the secret agreements for military equipment testify. Thus Cuba's greater knowledge of the area and understanding of the problems of development in a poor Third World state (though Cuba is a giant in comparison with Grenada) was a resource that it was able to employ successfully to persuade the Soviet Union to change its behaviour.

Although the Soviet Union and Cuba took different sides over the power struggle in the NJM, neither country played an active part, so far as we know, in the events themselves. Had the invasion not occurred in October 1983, Soviet and Cuban reactions to internal developments under Coard may have taken a different course. But that is something we can only speculate about. The basic lesson from the Soviet-Cuban link in Grenada is that Cuba can influence the Soviet Union. In Central America, Cuba has more in common with the unfolding revolutionary process, and so the potential for influencing Moscow is perhaps greater. I shall now turn to an examination of Soviet and Cuban policies in this region, with special reference to Nicaragua, in order to test this proposition.

Nicaragua

Central America has been in crisis for some seven years, and Nicaragua has become the main focus of US policy in the area. Since first taking office, President Reagan has had as one of his basic foreign-policy objectives the overthrow of the Sandinista government in Managua, on the grounds that it represents a threat to US national security interests. Reagan has acknowledged on a number of occasions that poverty and political and social inequalities are partly responsible for the revolutionary situation in Central America, but he also sees the hand of Moscow at work. His attempts to gain Congressional approval for US military aid for the Contras include, as David Durenberger, the Republican Chairman of the Senate Intelligence Committee, puts it, portraying anyone who votes against it as a 'stooge of communism'.[43] As revealed in the Iran-Contra link, Congress has even been bypassed to secure support for the Contras. The Soviet Union, using its Cuban 'pawn', is seen as the real threat in Nicaragua. In this section, the true nature of the threat should become evident.

The Nicaraguan revolution had an important impact on Soviet perceptions. The Sandinista victory seemed to support the long-held Cuban theory of revolution. Sergei Mikoyan, writing in the journal *Latinskaia Amerika* soon after the revolution, argued that the Sandinistas, like the 26 July Movement in Cuba, 'had shown (we may say now even proven) their capacity in certain conditions to substitute the political party of the proletariat in the role of the revolutionary vanguard'.[44] In Mikoyan's view, the most important objective of the revolution should be to guarantee power by gaining control over the state apparatus. The central task here was the building of a new type of army which would be faithful to the revolution. In economic policy he suggested pragmatism, with the NEP as the most applicable model.[45]

The scholarly literature in the Soviet Union gave far more significance to the Nicaraguan revolution than to events in Grenada. One Latin American specialist referred to the 'key' geostrategic, military-political position of Nicaragua in Central America and the Pacific and Atlantic Oceans.[46] Che Guevara was rehabilitated as the 'people's hero of America', and the size of Nicaragua (139,000 square kilometres) was compared to that of Czechoslovakia.[47] One author stated that 'Nicaragua is not Grenada', and saw the developments in Nicaragua as part of a 'regional process in which to some degree the peoples of all countries in the subregion are involved'.[48] Central America was now seen as the 'weakest link' of US imperialism in Latin America,[49] and great hope was placed in the Nicaraguan experience as an example to other states in the region.[50]

By the 1980s the Soviet Union and Cuba shared similar views on the revolutionary process in Latin America. However, this did not necessarily translate into identical or complementary policies. Cuba established diplomatic relations with the new regime in Managua in July 1979, and the Soviet Union followed suit in October.[51] This time, however, Cuba played no intermediary role; the Soviet ambassador in Mexico travelled to Managua to sign the official communiqué.[52] It should be noted at this stage that the Soviet Union did not provide any assistance to the Sandinistas during their struggle against Somoza. Cuba acted in an advisory capacity in trying to unite the different groups into a coherent fighting unit, but the material support it provided was actually less than that given by Costa Rica.[53] In fact, Castro was asked by the Sandinistas on three separate occasions in 1979 for more assistance, and each time he refused, saying, 'The best help we can give you is not to help you at all.'[54] Cuba and the Soviet Union shared the same sense of realism: any direct participation in Nicaragua would have risked a direct response from the United States.

Castro had become more cautious not only because of the danger of a US response to Cuban intervention, but also because of his interest in building diplomatic links with other Latin American states. As host to the 1979 Conference of the Non-Aligned Movement, he was more concerned about Cuba's position in the Third World, particularly in Latin America. The Soviet Union would also have opposed any Cuban intervention, for this would have led inevitably to a superpower crisis. Once the Sandinistas had seized power, however, both the Soviet Union and Cuba began to forge closer ties to the new government.

Cuba's commitment to the Sandinistas has always been relatively greater than the Soviet Union's, with Cuban personnel more directly involved in assisting the Sandinistas in a number of areas, including military training. The majority of Soviet scholars may have interpreted developments in Nicaragua very favourably, but the Soviet political leadership has not wanted to establish another 'Cuba', this time on the Latin American mainland. Cuba has been very costly to the Soviet treasury, and at a time of dwindling economic growth rates at home Moscow has become far less inclined to bail out the economies of those impoverished Third World states which are seemingly most prone to revolution.

Nevertheless, the first bilateral agreements between the Soviet Union and Nicaragua were signed in Moscow in March 1980: an agreement on economic and technical cooperation (covering mining, agriculture, energy, light and food industries, transport, communications and training of cadres), an agreement on air travel, and an agreement on cultural and scientific cooperation.[55] Since then there have been a number of other economic agreements, and by 1982 the volume of trade between the two countries exceeded that between the Soviet Union and Mexico.[56] However, Nicaragua's balance of trade with the USSR and other socialist states has shown a growing deficit. It exports coffee and sugar to the Soviet Union, but has become increasingly dependent on imports of Soviet oil and machinery. In 1984 total bilateral trade reached 138.5 million roubles, which was more than the combined volume of trade the Soviet Union had that year with Peru, Mexico, Colombia, Bolivia,

Panama, Ecuador and Venezuela.[57] Nicaragua has also been awarded observer status in the CMEA; it has received a large number of Soviet tanks and helicopters and therefore been able to build up the strongest armed forces in the region (it has a population onc fifth the size of Venezuela's, yet almost 20,000 more troops); and the FSLN has official party-to-party ties with the CPSU.[58]

The Cubans have supplied the Sandinistas with teachers (5,000 Cuban teachers gave instruction to some 250,000 Nicaraguan children between 1980 and 1984), doctors and military instructors.[59] Thus it appears that the Soviet Union and Cuba were again acting in concert, and dividing their labour in support of a friendly revolutionary government. The Cubans did not need to convince the Soviet leadership of the political importance of Nicaragua, as they had to do of Grenada. Yet, although the Soviet Union's trade with Nicaragua has increased dramatically in percentage terms, it is still little more than a drop in the ocean. The trade statistics cited above are only further evidence of the extremely small amount of Soviet trade with Latin America. The Soviet Union has not traditionally traded much with other Latin American states, despite its long-held desire to strengthen economic links with such countries as Mexico, and this is due largely to a lack of complementarity between the Soviet and Latin American economies.[60] Much has been made of Nicaragua's status as an observer in the CMEA,[61] but it has not resulted in large levels of aid from the socialist-bloc countries. One should remember that Mexico, too, has enjoyed a similar status in the Council, yet the Soviet Union has not therefore helped it solve its massive economic problems.[62] Of the socialist countries, Cuba has been the most generous aid donor to Nicaragua, despite the shaky state of its own economy. By the end of 1982, Cuban aid was valued at $286 million.[63] Mexico also gave more material assistance to the Sandinistas during their first years in power than the Soviet Union (as indeed did the United States).[64]

It should not be surprising that Castro's commitment to the Sandinistas is stronger than that of the Soviet Union. The Cuban leadership has always been far more ideologically committed to supporting revolution in the Third World. In view of its long history of involvement in Africa in support of national liberation movements, it was Cuba's duty to support a nearby revolutionary government in an area of vital importance to its own security and political interests. The Caribbean Basin, however, is of little significance to Moscow's global security calculations. Soviet scholars may have been enthusiastic about the events in Central America – many of them in 1981 expected the 'final offensive' in El Salvador to result in a victory for the guerrillas – but those who have to make policy in the Kremlin take a more realistic and pragmatic approach. During the early 1980s, the increased tension between East and West, declining economic growth rates, and the rapid succession of leaders as one followed another to a grave behind Lenin's mausoleum, combined to force a re-evaluation of Soviet foreign policy towards the Third World.

Brezhnev's last years in the Kremlin were marked by stagnation and corruption. As Soviet economic growth rates dwindled, the costs of maintaining a much-expanded presence in the Third World rapidly rose. The bailing out of the Vietnamese economy since the withdrawal of the Americans in the mid-1970s has created a heavy burden on the Soviet Union (an estimated $1 million a day).[65] The economic, military and political costs of Afghanistan since the Soviet invasion of that country have also taken their toll. Yet, for geostrategic reasons, the Soviet leadership has shown a much greater willingness to expend large resources on these two states than it has on Central America or the Caribbean. Whereas Nicaragua was given observer status in the CMEA (Grenada of course did not even get this), Vietnam has been a full member of the socialist bloc's economic community since 1978. That same year the Soviet Union signed a 25-year Treaty of Friendship and Cooperation with Vietnam. All other such treaties that the Soviet Union has concluded with Third World states have had a duration of only 15 or 20 years; such is the importance it attaches to Vietnam.[66] Nicaragua does not have a Treaty of Friendship and Cooperation with the Soviet Union, but then neither does Cuba. It would seem that the USSR is reluctant to give any form of written security guarantee to a country outside its direct sphere of influence.

However, the level of Soviet support for the Sandinistas *has* risen, and this increase can be explained as a response to hostile reactions in the United States to the Nicaraguan revolution – including economic and military pressure exerted through the Contras – rather than by any Cuban influence, as in the case of Grenada.[67] There is no evidence, though, that Moscow intends to give any sort of military guarantee to the Sandinistas, or that it would intervene with Soviet, or Cuban proxy, troops at any level of escalation in the conflict.

Nevertheless, between 1983 and 1986, it provided sufficient arms and economic aid to the Sandinistas not only to signify its support, but also to tie the United States down in its own backyard.

This low-risk strategy provides certain benefits for the Soviet Union at relatively little cost. Reports in *Pravda* and *Izvestiia* of US policy towards Nicaragua since 1980 have stressed the problems this policy has created for Reagan domestically, with both Congress and US public opinion.[68] Gorbachev's foreign-policy strategy has involved a careful balancing-act between public support for a negotiated solution to the Central American crisis through the Contadora process, and a commitment to provide the Sandinistas with enough arms to ensure they are able to continue the war – but without taking the risk that more direct Soviet engagement would entail. Even when Soviet ships were mined in Nicaraguan harbours, an operation organized by the CIA, the Soviet reaction was restrained and restricted to diplomatic complaints.[69] One of Gorbachev's aims is to divert attention from his own problems in Afghanistan. As long as the war rages in Nicaragua, the United States can be depicted as a danger to international stability. In addition, he hopes both to encourage mass movements in the United States that will put pressure on the Reagan administration to moderate its policy, and to strengthen anti-American sentiment in Western Europe, where US policy on this issue is generally opposed.[70]

Although Central America itself is distant and strategically unimportant for the Soviet Union, US policies there threaten to weaken the unity of the Atlantic Alliance, the European part of which is of special significance to Moscow. Furthermore, US policy in Central America undermines the USA's credibility and standing with those more important Third World actors, such as Mexico, with which Gorbachev wishes to establish much closer ties. Soviet foreign policy under Gorbachev may have become more multipolar in focus, compared with the dominantly bipolar Brezhnev era, when US-Soviet relations were top of the agenda, but the new General-Secretary realizes that, in order to conduct a multipolar foreign policy, he first has to wean the most important Third World states away from Washington's embrace. In fact, despite the claim made by some scholars regarding a new 'multipolar' foreign-policy strategy under Gorbachev, actual Soviet behaviour since his rise to power suggests the bipolar focus is still dominant. The competition with the United States has simply assumed a different strategy.[71] Soviet policy in Central America should be seen in this light.

The Nicaraguans receive large amounts of Soviet arms, but cannot look forward to anywhere near the same level of economic support that Moscow provides for Cuba (a legacy of a different era in Soviet foreign policy). The new Soviet leadership since the death of Brezhnev has made this clear. It was Andropov, during his brief tenure as General-Secretary, who first signalled a change in Soviet foreign policy towards socialist-oriented states in the Third World. Andropov stated that the Soviet Union would help such states on the road to socialist development only as far as its resources would allow, stressing that they must attain their goal largely under their own steam.[72] Gorbachev has continued this policy which, far more significantly, has now been given official sanction by its incorporation into the new Party Programme published in 1986.[73]

Meanwhile, the Cuban commitment to Nicaragua's economic and political development continues, for Nicaragua is of great importance to Cuba's foreign-policy priorities, centred as they are on the Third World and Latin American solidarity. For Cuba, Nicaragua is by far the most important international development since its own revolution of 1959. Although some Soviet scholars see it in a similar light, those who make the decisions in the Kremlin attach importance to Nicaragua only in so far it furthers Soviet interests in its new competitive strategy with the United States. In these terms, support for the Sandinista revolution comes way down on the foreign-policy agenda.

In terms of the influence relationship between the Soviet Union and Cuba, there is again no evidence of direct pressure being applied on either side. Both, for their own reasons, some of which coincide and some not, have given support to the Sandinistas. There has been no large-scale intervention of Cuban troops, and no Soviet military personnel have engaged in combat operations, either before, during or after the revolution. Cuba's greater sense of realism in its foreign policy, a product of its earlier experiences in Africa and Latin America, has led it to take a far more pragmatic approach in its support for the Sandinistas. It has been careful not to give the United States a justification for direct military intervention. Castro has given his support to the Contadora process – which was established by Colombia, Mexico, Panama and Venezuela – and has stated on a number of occasions that the civil war in El Salvador can only be resolved through a negotiated peaceful settlement.[74] The Soviet Union supports these positions too, but it is interesting to note that Moscow came later than Havana to supporting Contadora. Cuba has been more concerned with preserving the Nicaraguan revolution; Moscow with preserving an uncomfortable and troublesome conflict in the USA's backyard. The Soviet Union gave its full support to the peace process only when its international image would have been damaged if it had not done so, and when it was convinced that the guerrillas in El Salvador were not about to achieve a military victory. Cuba did not persuade the Soviet Union to change its policy; changing circumstances did.

With regard to Soviet and Cuban influence over the Sandinistas, it is clear that the Cubans are far more important than the Soviets. In reply to US claims that the USSR was responsible for events in Central America, Castro stated somewhat indignantly that 'the Soviet Union has had nothing whatsoever to do with Latin America ... The Soviets did not know even one of the present leaders of Nicaragua.'[75] He went on to argue that the same was true of the revolutionaries in El Salvador and Guatemala. Castro knew the revolutionary leaders in each of these states personally, and Cuba and he provided the role models for other Latin American revolutionary movements, not the Soviet Union. Tomás Borge, one of the Sandinista leaders, has acknowledged that this is the case in Nicaragua: 'I won't deny that the Cuban Revolution has exerted a certain positive influence ... The influence of the USSR is rather more remote.'[76] Borge has strongly denied accusations that Nicaragua is being turned into a Soviet 'satellite', stating that, on the contrary, the Sandinistas would rather have economic and trade relations with their most natural market – the United States.[77]

In summary it can be stated that, as in Angola, Soviet and Cuban policies towards the Sandinistas developed largely independently of one another, but ultimately converged without influence or leverage being applied by either side. If either party did influence the other, it would have been Cuba influencing the Soviet Union – not the other way around – although all we have to go on is circumstantial evidence and the fact that the Soviet Union shifted its policy till it was more in keeping with Cuba's. However, the priorities of the two sides were very different and were reflected in the relative amounts of economic aid they gave to Nicaragua. While it is possible that a rational policy for Castro would have been to ensure that the

Sandinistas did not, by asking for Soviet aid, threaten Cuba's slice of the aid cake, it is more likely that Castro would have lobbied the Soviet Union on their behalf. We do not know if this was done, or to what extent it was successful. However, what can be assumed is that Cuba, though by far the weaker power of the two, has more political and ideological influence in the Caribbean and Central America than the Soviet Union, and is more willing to employ it. In Central America Cuba is certainly not a puppet or surrogate, but follows an independent foreign policy to further its own perceived interests.

8

CONCLUSIONS AND POLICY IMPLICATIONS

Having examined the historical development of Soviet-Cuban relations, and the way this relationship has operated in specific situations, I shall draw a number of conclusions before going on to assess the policy implications for West European governments.

First, the relationship which developed between the two states was certainly not an inevitable consequence of the Cuban revolution. Given the history of US policy towards Cuba since the Spanish-American war and Washington's support for Batista, Castro's revolution was bound to take on a strong element of 'anti-Yankee-ism' in its initial stages. However, this should not be equated simplistically with a desire on the part of those guerrillas who seized power in 1959 to construct a Marxist-Leninist political system and forge close ties with the Soviet Union. There were of course some, mainly in the old PSP, who did advocate such a course, but at the outset they were in a minority. It was largely the US response to the revolution (the abrogation of an agreement to purchase Cuban sugar, the refusal to refine oil, a trade embargo and the Bay of Pigs) which strengthened these tendencies in Havana and ultimately left Castro with little option but to turn to the Soviet Union in order to ensure the survival of his nationalist revolution.

Second, neither the Soviet Union nor Cuba is responsible for creating the conditions which lead to conflict and revolution in the Third World. Neither country instigated the civil war in Angola; rather, they were drawn in, as were other external actors, by a process of action/reaction as the indigenous groups sought foreign assistance. In the Horn of Africa, the military coups which brought socialist-oriented regimes to power were not the product of Cuban or Soviet interference, but the result of domestic power struggles. When it was evident that Somalia and Ethiopia were heading towards a major war over the disputed Ogaden territory, both Castro and Podgorny sought a political solution to the conflict. Neither the New Jewel Movement in Grenada nor the Sandinistas in Nicaragua can thank Cuba or the Soviet Union for playing any decisive role in their bids for power. In short, the Soviet-Cuban link has not been the cause of revolution and conflict in regional crises; rather, these have been the result of local factors rooted in historical ethnic rivalries or socio-economic circumstances.

Third, Cuba does not act as a Soviet pawn. The Soviet Union's much greater power and Cuba's heavy economic dependence have not given Moscow complete leverage or influence over Havana's foreign policies. Indeed, in the Caribbean Basin, Cuban influence has if anything tended to make the Soviet Union change its behaviour. This was certainly the case in Grenada, as revealed in the secret documents that were discovered by the invading forces in 1983. It is possible, too, that the Cuban experience and some persuasion from the Cubans helped to change Soviet perceptions and policies towards Nicaragua. Cuban policy towards Angola was at the outset conducted independently of Moscow, and was more consistent than that of the Soviet Union from the 1960s right through the civil war. In the Horn of Africa, however, the two countries acted in tight coordination from the beginning in a jointly organized strategy of intervention. In this last case Cuba may have been influenced by the Soviet Union, but even here Soviet leverage was not sufficient to compel Cuban troops to suppress the Eritrean rebels. Although it is extremely difficult to measure and identify influence, the evidence points to the conclusion that influence relations between the Soviet Union and Cuba are a two-way process.

Fourth, the Soviet Union and Cuba have different hierarchies of interests. Moscow has traditionally viewed the world in East-West terms, and its foreign-policy priorities lie in the USA, Europe, Asia and the Middle East. Latin America is of little economic or strategic interest. Soviet foreign policy in the Third World should be seen in terms of competition with the capitalist West and the overall correlation of forces. Cuba under Castro has traditionally viewed the world in North-South terms, and its major foreign-policy

77

concerns lie in the Third World, with Latin America having the greatest priority. Cuban foreign policy should be seen in terms of Castro's commitment to restructuring international economic relations and to reversing the unequal economic relationship between the industrialized North and the underdeveloped South.

Fifth, both Soviet and Cuban perceptions, policies, strategies and hierachies of interests change over time, either as a response to events or, as we are once again witnessing in the USSR, because of a change in political leadership. It is mistaken, then, to view Soviet and Cuban foreign policies and Soviet-Cuban relations in the 1980s as if we were still in the 1960s. Cuba, like the Soviet Union, will support a revolutionary regime once it has achieved power, but there has been a significant change in Castro's thinking on the feasibility of 'exporting' revolution. Cuba still provides training for revolutionaries and backs the guerrillas in El Salvador, but Castro has become far more cautious in the kind of support he gives. He acknowledges that in the first years of the Cuban revolution he and his comrades were 'arrogant, idealistic, and even chauvinistic'; now, in the 1980s, he has not only toned down his revolutionary rhetoric, but no longer sends Cubans to fight in other Latin American revolutions.[1] He supports a political solution to the conflict in El Salvador through the Contadora peace process, and cautions the Sandinistas against too rapid a move towards socialism. Cuba now has diplomatic relations with over 120 states, and Castro's personal commitment in the 1980s is not to armed guerrilla struggle in the Third World, but to the New International Economic Order.

It is likewise a misperception to look upon Soviet foreign policy as being incapable of change. Most Western scholars and politicians now accept that the totalitarian model of the Soviet Union is no longer applicable, if it ever was. This study has shown that Soviet policy towards the Third World has become increasingly pragmatic. For example, the current leadership in the Kremlin may interpret events in Nicaragua in a positive light, but Gorbachev has made it clear that the Soviet Union does not want any more economically burdensome Cubas.

Assessing costs and benefits

The benefits to the Soviet Union of its relationship with Cuba should not be exaggerated. The Caribbean Basin is important for

Western security in that it is one of the principal supply routes between America and Europe. In the event of conflict in the European theatre, it could become vital. Thus facilities for Soviet naval deployments in Cuba are clearly a strategic gain for Moscow in an area perceived as critical to US security interests. However, the 1962 agreement between the superpowers prohibits the placing of Soviet offensive weapons in Cuba, and in 1970 the Soviet Union refrained from constructing a naval base at Cienfuegos in conformity with this agreement. The USSR has long-range submarines, so the presence of a Soviet strike-force in the Caribbean does not depend on Cuba, but it is clearly useful and convenient to have friendly ports of call so close to the United States.

Another benefit for the Soviet Union, related to the strategic issue, is a large intelligence-gathering centre just outside Havana. This is obviously useful for monitoring US naval and troop movements, but the increasing sophistication of modern communications technology has made it less important today than it was a decade ago.

As documented above in the case studies, the participation of Cuban combat troops in regional conflicts has been decisive to outcomes favoured by the Soviet Union. There can be no doubt that the cooperative intervention strategy in Angola and the Horn of Africa was seen in Moscow as a major benefit stemming from its relationship with Havana.

In the ideological realm, too, the Cuban connection has paid the Soviet Union dividends. Castro was a revolutionary before he was a communist, and his ultimate adoption of a Marxist-Leninist political system, modelled on that of the USSR, served as an example to other Third World states – at least this was the initial Soviet perception. Under Castro, Cuba has made notable progress in the sphere of public welfare. If one measures progress not by GNP or other economic indicators, but by what is termed the 'physical quality of life index' (e.g., infant mortalities, life expectancy, health care and educational levels), then Cuba compares favourably with Western industrialized nations. In this respect Cuba has supposedly made the Soviet model of development more attractive to other Third World revolutionary and nationalist leaders. This was certainly how the Brezhnev leadership saw it. Cuba also demonstrated that the Soviet Union was a legitimate global actor and that there was no area in the world where it could not develop close ties and allies.

In the diplomatic field Cuba was seen as an asset in the 1970s in the bid to persuade other Third World states that Moscow was the natural ally of the less developed world. Castro's leading position in the Non-Aligned Movement during this period was seen in a very positive light; as the Third World became more important in the United Nations, the Soviet Union found it useful to have a close friend – in both the NAM and the UN – supporting its own foreign-policy goals.

Although these benefits are substantial, they look less impressive when weighed up against the costs. One should bear in mind that the relationship between the two states began in the early 1960s, when the Soviet Union had high economic growth rates and Khrushchev was pursuing a strategy of wooing radical Third World regimes by offering enormous amounts of aid and credit. It was during this period that the Soviet Union began supplying free military equipment to Cuba, purchasing Cuban sugar at above world market prices, supplying oil at below world market prices, and providing Castro with long-term credit. It is not clear precisely how much Cuba costs the Soviet Union, but the CIA estimates that in the 1980s the figure has been over $4 billion a year. While these figures are almost certainly inflated (for example, subsidies paid for in soft currency are translated into US dollars), it is nevertheless evident that Cuba is very costly to the Soviet Union at a time of steadily declining Soviet economic growth.

Since the early 1980s (i.e., before the rise of Gorbachev), Soviet Third World specialists and officials have been advocating a shift in policy towards the more dynamic capitalist-oriented Third World states, for the sake of mutual economic advantage. This was clearly stated in a *Pravda* article by Karen Brutents, Deputy Head of the International Department, in 1982.[2] Soviet Latin Americanists have also been articulating support for a new strategy aimed at the larger states in the continent, such as Mexico, Brazil and Argentina. One proponent of this line is Viktor Volskii, head of Moscow's Latin American Institute.[3] Although the specialist literature and official statements do not directly refer to the economic burden of Cuba, criticism of this burden is often implicit. Further evidence of Moscow's concern about the costs of its relationship with Cuba can be deduced from Gorbachev's new policies, a subject I take up below.

There have also been significant political costs. In the 1970s, when Brezhnev's primary objective was to develop a new relationship with the United States, Soviet-Cuban activities in regional conflicts in Africa undermined the whole detente process. The Soviet Union may have thought that it was acting in accordance with the Basic Principles Agreement, but events in Angola and the Horn were perceived in Washington as breaking the spirit of detente. In addition, in 1979 the 'mini crisis' over the Soviet brigade in Cuba helped to spoil the prospects for Congressional ratification of the SALT II Treaty.

By the early 1980s it was acknowledged by many in the Soviet Union that, despite its impressive record in some areas, such as health care, Cuba was not proving to be an economic model for emulation by other countries. Its economy was suffering because of structural defects inherent in the political system. (The same was of course true of the Soviet Union, and this too was recognized.)[4] Furthermore, not only was the Cuban developmental model not going to attract other nationalist leaders in the Third World; the promise that Castro would persuade the Non-Aligned Movement that Moscow was its natural ally was not fulfilled. Indeed, it was Castro's support for the Soviet invasion of Afghanistan that lost him his credibility in the movement. In sum, Moscow's links with Cuba carry substantial economic and political costs which, when measured against the gains, have provided Gorbachev with a salutory lesson in his dealings with other radical regimes in the Third World.

The gains for Cuba from the bilateral relationship are far more substantial, if not critical. Cuba relies upon the Soviet Union for economic assistance to ensure its viability, and for military supplies to ensure its security. These are the two core interests of any state in the international system, and without the Soviet Union it is difficult to envisage how Cuba could possibly survive and maintain its present form of government. The relationship has also benefited Castro in his personal commitment to national liberation movements and to what he sees as assisting the poor, underdeveloped Third World states in their attempts to break out of their dependence on the capitalist countries. Cuba's commitment to African liberation movements began soon after the Cuban revolution in 1959, but the cooperative strategy of intervention in Angola and the Horn of Africa, in which the Soviet Union assisted Cuba in sending combat troops, furthered Castro's foreign-policy goals as well as those of Moscow.

The costs for Cuba of its relationship with the Soviet Union are greater in potential than in practice. The huge gap in military capabilities is of little significance, since geography and the certain US response dictate that Moscow would not seek to 'stabilize' Cuba, as it has stabilized East European states, by a military intervention in the event of Cuba's 'defection'. But if developments in Cuba were not to Moscow's liking, the economic weapon is always there and, if applied, could have a devastating effect. It could be that Cuba's relationship with Moscow has resulted in political isolation in the very region that is of the most importance to Castro, Latin America. However, it was not Castro's ties with Moscow that other Latin American governments objected to in the 1960s so much as his commitment to exporting revolution, which the Soviet leadership also opposed. Since Castro moderated his views on the export of revolution in the 1970s, Cuba has re-established diplomatic relations with many Latin American states, including most recently Brazil. Rather than subverting governments in Latin America, Castro is now strengthening political and economic links with the most important states in the area, and his relationship with Moscow has not served to undermine this process.

One significant consequence of the Soviet-Cuban relationship has been Cuba's loss of position in the Non-Aligned Movement. Castro's endorsement of the Soviet invasion of Afghanistan in 1979, when he was chairman of the NAM, proved to many Third World states the fiction of Cuba's non-aligned status. Cuba was faced with an apparent dilemma in the United Nations and had to choose between voting with the Soviet Union and the socialist bloc or showing solidarity with the Third World. That Cuba chose to vote with the USSR is evidence perhaps of an acknowledged responsibility, in the face of adversity, to show allegiance to the socialist bloc. It was not a straightforward North-South issue. It was also an East-West issue, and in the event Castro felt obliged, despite misgivings, to remain loyal to Moscow. As a result, Cuba lost not only the support of the Third World for a seat on the UN Security Council (the chairman of the Non-Aligned Movement should have elicited such support), but also a good deal of prestige in an arena close to Castro's heart. Castro could have abstained on the UN vote, and the reason he chose not to could be explained in part by a fear of Soviet retaliation in the form of cuts in aid, as had occurred in the late 1960s.

In weighing up the costs and benefits for both sides in the bilateral relationship, what is clear is that Cuba is far less important to the Soviet Union than the Soviet Union is to Cuba. Ultimately the only significant reason for the continuation of Soviet commitment is the question of prestige. Too many resources have already been spent over a long period for the Soviet Union to give up on Cuba now. If it did so, it would be admitting the failure of Soviet-type socialism in the Western hemisphere. However, as already noted, changes can and do occur in Soviet and Cuban policies, so a brief assessment should be made of the likely course of Soviet-Cuban relations in the late 1980s and beyond. Any appropriate West European strategy requires a proper understanding of the probable future of this relationship.

Soviet-Cuban relations under Gorbachev
It is a widely held assumption that new political leaders make a difference, and a number of academic studies have adequately demonstrated that a change in leadership correlates with changes in public policy, in socialist as well as capitalist states.[5] It is evident that under Gorbachev the Soviet Union is in the process of reassessing its foreign-policy commitments and strategies, and that no area is being excluded, not even Cuba. Furthermore, it has been possible to identify a new trend in Gorbachev's general foreign-policy strategy towards the Third World up to the end of 1986. In a number of speeches he has made it plain that his basic objective is the reconstruction of the Soviet domestic economy. This priority has led to radical economic and political reforms in the Soviet Union, to radical arms control proposals, and to a change in Soviet policy towards the Third World. The Soviet Union will no longer be willing to prop up socialist-oriented regimes with large injections of economic aid. Instead, Gorbachev is courting the more dynamic capitalist-oriented Third World states in order to develop mutually advantageous economic relations. This is in line with the policy that many Soviet Third World specialists have been advocating for a number of years.

Cuba's special position as a member of the CMEA and the world socialist system is reflected in the Soviet-Cuban trade and aid agreement of April 1986, which includes $3 billion of new credits between 1986 and 1990, a substantial increase over the previous five-year period. However, the Cuban economy is in a critical condition for a number of reasons, many of which lie outside the control of the Cuban government. Hurricanes and drought have seriously damaged the sugar harvest, and the fall in the world market price for sugar has depleted hard-currency earnings. In the past, Cuba has relied on the reselling of surplus Soviet oil, delivered at well below the world market price, for a large portion of its hard-currency receipts. The sharp fall in oil prices in 1986 meant that Cuba lost $3 million. Currently Cuba actually pays above the world market price for oil, while the price the Soviet Union pays for Cuban sugar is pegged for the next five years at approximately 1985 prices.

The Soviet Union is not about to give up on its commitment to Cuba, but Gorbachev does want to reduce the present level of aid. He is in the process of putting his own house in order, and would like to see Castro do the same, for he too is beset with many of the problems that the Soviet Union faces (problems common to any Leninist system). Bureaucratism, inertia, corruption and a lack of initiative are some of the difficulties that both leaders recognize they need to overcome. In his speech to the Third Party Congress in Havana in February 1986, Ligachev, the Kremlin number two, noted with satisfaction that 'Cuban communists are not resting on their laurels', but seeking to rectify the situation.[6] However, it is interesting to note the different approach the two party leaders are taking to overcome similar problems. Whereas Gorbachev is advocating decentralization of decision-making, giving some autonomy to local enterprises and appealing to economic instincts by allowing at least some private enterprise, Castro is tightening up on labour discipline and using moral incentives.

At the reconvened second session of the Third Party Congress in December 1986, Castro repeatedly referred to the dangers of 'filling people's heads with material aspirations', stating that he was opposed to using the term 'standard of living', since it could 'unleash a terrible national selfishness'. For Castro economic incentives to stimulate production carry the dangerous potential of fostering a capitalist mentality, and in a telling point in his speech he argued: 'Do those who think only of economic mechanisms and economic accounting really believe socialism can be built on that alone. This was an ideological mistake ... even if they do know Karl Marx's *Capital* off by heart.'[7] Castro was opposed to the developments in Czechoslovakia in 1968, and, although the new Soviet reforms do not yet go that far, he does appear to be unwilling to copy Gorbachev's economic strategy in Cuba.

Meanwhile, he has promised to speed up the completion of construction projects financed by the USSR, he has abolished the experiment with private peasant markets, and he has instituted a number of austerity measures: electricity prices up by 40%, public transport prices up by 100%, and some cuts in subsidies on basic food products. If these and other measures fail to improve the Cuban economy, Gorbachev may not be willing to continue increasing Soviet aid (as has been the pattern since the 1960s), and this could lead to renewed tensions between the two states.

Another area of possible future tension lies in the respective attitudes and policies both states have towards North-South issues, and in particular towards the Latin American debt and the call for a New International Economic Order (NIEO). At a meeting in Havana to mark the twenty-fifth anniversary of the establishment of Soviet-Cuban relations, Soviet Politburo member Solomentsev stated that 'the most important international duty of our party ... is growth in the (Soviet) economy, the well-being of the Soviet people, and strengthening the national security of the country'.[8] At the Twenty-seventh Party Congress in Moscow, Castro's speech focused upon hunger, poverty and underdevelopment in the Third World, and called upon the Soviet Union to support the demands for the NIEO. Cuba was one of the first states to advocate a restructuring of international economic relations along the lines of the NIEO, and in recent years Castro has focused more attention on this subject and the Latin American debt than on any other issue in international politics. The Soviet Union gives only lip service to the call for the NIEO. Castro has argued passionately that the Latin American debt cannot and should not be repaid, whereas Gorbachev, in his Congress speech of 1986, stated that there should be a political solution to the debt crisis.

Castro has organized a number of conferences in Havana on the Latin American debt at which he has argued that there are 'no such things as technical formulas', and that the only way to resolve the crisis is through the 'result of our peoples' struggles'.[9] He has also made it clear that the Soviet Union is considered in this context to be part of the industrialized North: 'I don't think it's only the former colonial powers that have this obligation; I believe that all of the countries that in one way or another have achieved the privilege of development have this elementary duty.'[10] The 'duty' is to accept non-payment of the debt and to restructure the international economy to benefit the Third World. Gorbachev recognizes the increasing interdependence in global politics and economics, and the need to overcome the debt problem, but given his new domestic and foreign economic strategy, he is unlikely to give serious support to Castro's proposals.

Although there is potential for tensions with Gorbachev at the helm in the Kremlin, the two states do gain significant benefits from their relationship, and these should be sufficient to ensure that any strains that develop will be manageable. One can speculate, however, about the future of Soviet-Cuban relations after Castro. While it is impossible to predict anything with any certainty, it could well be that without the personalized leadership of this charismatic revolutionary figure, a more collective leadership will emerge which will have stronger institutionalized ties with Moscow. Fidel's brother Raúl is the designated heir, but one should bear in mind that there is only a couple of years difference in age between them. The revolution has bureaucratized the institutional structures of the party apparatus, and many members of the emerging elite, who will eventually take over important positions in the party, were educated and trained in the Soviet Union and have close ties with elites in Moscow. There is now one party member for every twenty Cuban citizens, and, as Castro has noted, there are 3,500 party members for every one of those who took part in the struggle against Batista.[11] At a closed session of the recent Party Congress in which Castro attacked certain tendencies in the party, he apparently met with opposition from a group of technocrats 'with strong sympathies for and professional connections with the Soviet Union'.[12] It could also be argued that the Revolutionary Armed Forces may emerge as a challenge to party supremacy and engage in more international revolutionary activity in regional conflicts. Yet it is more likely that the party will be strong enough to control the military, and that a more bureaucratic and technocratic approach will develop which will restrict costly military adventures overseas and concentrate on domestic economic problems.

Castro has always been a fervent nationalist; after studying law, his early training was as a revolutionary guerrilla fighter. Much of Cuban foreign policy, particularly the support for national liberation struggles in Africa and Latin America, can be explained by his personality and revolutionary zeal. But even Castro, faced with the realities of global politics, has toned down his revolutionary idealism and become more pragmatic and realistic in his foreign-policy behaviour. Cuba is most likely to become even more of a status quo actor when Fidel departs the scene, and its links with the Soviet Union could well be strengthened. But this depends in part on other external actors; so finally I shall turn to an assessment of the policy options for West European governments in their relations with the Soviet Union and Cuba.

Policy implications

Given the five conclusions noted above, and given the present uncertain state of Soviet-Cuban relations, what are the policy implications for Western Europe? It should be recognized at the outset that the Soviet-Cuban link in international relations does not have a high priority in the hierarchy of foreign-policy concerns in European capitals, and that Latin America is not of direct strategic concern to Europe, as it is to the United States. Thus any European role will be constrained by the limited influence Europe has in both the USSR and Cuba. However, the Soviet-Cuban link in regional conflicts has led to increasing tensions between East and West. As part of the West, it is in Europe's interests to use its limited influence to discourage such future actions of cooperative intervention and therefore avoid their negative consequences for East-West relations.

I have noted how Cuba has become less of a direct revolutionary challenge to the status quo, how it now supports a diplomatic solution to the crisis in Central America and to the conflict in Southern Africa, and how it acts independently of the Soviet Union. Given these facts, and the parlous state of the Cuban economy, now would be an opportune moment for Western governments to foster closer political and economic ties with Havana. Cuba is of course so tightly integrated into the Eastern bloc's economic system, and is so dependent on the Soviet Union for its economic survival, that there is little point in trying to wean Castro away from Moscow. But by taking up recent Cuban offers to invest in collaborative projects,

Western Europe could reduce the level of this dependence. Furthermore, closer political and economic relations would probably encourage the Cuban government to exercise more restraint in its international behaviour. The presence of Western investments would mean it had more to lose by engaging in adventures overseas. As Gorbachev is well aware, the Soviet Union is unable to compete effectively with the West in the technological realm, so Western technology has clear advantages and attractions for Third World states. Cuba is no exception. It may not be the most attractive proposition for Western investors, but if European governments encouraged and provided inducements to business enterprises to establish collaborative ventures there, Moscow's potential leverage over Cuba could ultimately be weakened. Creating stronger political and economic ties now could pay dividends in post-Castro Cuba.

West European governments should recognize the indigenous roots of civil war and regional conflicts, and should encourage political solutions whenever a military strategy runs the risk of drawing in the Soviet Union and/or Cuba as suppliers of military equipment and advisers. For example, in the case of Central America, if a diplomatic as opposed to military solution were seriously attempted, the Soviet Union would have no role to play, for it is principally as an arms supplier to the Sandinistas that Moscow has gained any influence in the region. Neighbouring countries have good reason to fear that any intensification of the conflicts in Nicaragua and El Salvador could, if the regional arms race continues apace, eventually spill over and destabilize them. Thus they are the external actors most suited to the role of intermediary. Colombia, Mexico, Panama and Venezuela have provided the framework – Contadora – for a potential regional diplomatic solution. It should be borne in mind that each of these states shares Washington's concern about containing Soviet and Cuban influence in Latin America. Contadora is thus a vehicle which could be employed to exclude the Soviet Union from any meaningful participation in the politics of the region. If the conflict can be resolved through peaceful means, the major access route for Soviet influence – military supplies – would no longer be open.

Europe should act as far as possible as a single voice, using the institutions of the European Community (EC); for only a united 'European' approach can hope to have any influence. Western Europe could encourage regional integration and cooperation among the Central American states, including Nicaragua. If inter-governmental or supranational organizations were to be established, the EC could reward Central America with preferential trade agreements. Britain and the other EC states should strengthen their economic, cultural and political ties with the governments of the region, again including the Nicaraguan government. Cuba in the early 1960s, in a Cold War international environment, had little choice but to turn to the Soviet Union for economic assistance. In the 1980s European governments are in a better position to act independently and not to isolate Nicaragua, thus forcing it into the hands of Moscow. We know from history that radical nationalism does not necessarily equal Soviet-type socialism. The Nicaraguan revolution was essentially nationalist in its origins. We also know that negative Western reactions to radical nationalism in the Third World can increase the likelihood of the eventual development of Soviet-type socialism. Given the very strong commitment to plural-ism among large sections of Nicaraguan society, and the desire of the Sandinistas to gain international legitimacy, Britain and the other countries of Western Europe should do all they can to promote a diplomatic solution to the war, which is the single most important factor militating against both pluralism and legitimacy. The EC should therefore continue to give its strongest backing to Contadora and its Support Group.

Britain and other West European states have closer ties and interests in Southern Africa; so there is a greater prospect here for a more effective European role. Although the Soviet Union and Cuba have both won allies in the region, Moscow has not been able to gain complete influence and leverage over its client states. It was the United States that acted as intermediary in the non-aggression pacts of 1984 between South Africa and Angola, and South Africa and Mozambique. The Soviet Union opposed these developments and was excluded from participating in them. The EC should use its influence to encourage a political solution to the conflict in Angola, not by supporting UNITA, but by actively cooperating with the MPLA government with the objective of achieving Namibian independence and linking this to the withdrawal of Cuban troops from Angola. The USSR is a vital actor in Southern Africa only because of the military requirements of some Front Line states; the economies of both Angola and Mozambique are still much more closely tied to the West than to the socialist bloc. So again, in order to deal with the Soviet-Cuban link in Southern Africa, it is necessary first to recognize the local causes of conflict, and then to encourage a diplomatic solution, which would weaken Moscow's position (as arms supplier).

European governments should express their concern directly at the way Soviet-Cuban cooperative interventions in the Third World heighten the overall level of tensions between East and West. Any such deterioration in East-West relations also damages their own bilateral links with the USSR and Cuba. As well as individually, they should express their concern through the institutions of the EC, since Gorbachev has been more willing than previous Soviet leaders to deal with the Community as a legitimate political and economic actor. Europe is important to Moscow, and although the Soviet-Cuban link may not be of direct primary significance to Europe, we could, through quiet diplomacy in our dealings with Moscow, help to moderate the propensity of this link to manifest itself in adventures in the Third World.

Now that Spain is a member of the EC, Madrid could play an important part in promoting a more moderate Cuban foreign policy. Spain has strong historical, linguistic and cultural ties with Latin America, and its own non-violent transition from dictatorship to democracy gives it the credentials for playing an active diplomatic ro towards Cuba. During the recent visit of the Spanish Prime Minister to Havana, it is notable that Castro granted a request he made for the release of a political prisoner.

The West is much more likely to gain concessions from Cuba, even under Castro, if Western governments pursue a hard-headed policy through direct political and economic ties with Havana. The irony will not be lost on anyone who has visited the island that despite the anti-American rhetoric articulated by Fidel, and the close relationship with the USSR, most Cubans seem to prefer Americans to Russians. Also, the English language is more widely studied than Russian. This is not to say that the majority of Cubans would like to see a return to capitalism and US hegemony – for that is manifestly not the case. It is to say, though, that if the United States were to overcome its long-held ideological bias against Cuba and engage in serious negotiations with Castro's government, some accommodation could be reached between the two antagonists (for this is what they will remain) which could lead to a formal (or tacit) agreement regarding security in the Caribbean Basin and Central America. All revolutions have eventually come to accept and abide by the norms of interstate behaviour. By an active strategy of political and economic engagement with both the USSR and Cuba, Europe could help to further this process in relation to the Soviet-Cuban link.

NOTES

Chapter 1

1 *The Soviet-Cuban Connection in Central America and the Caribbean* (Washington, D.C., 1985). Released by the Departments of State and Defense.

2 See, for example, Steven Lukes, *Power: A Radical View* (London, Macmillan, 1979).

3 Robert A. Dahl, 'The concept of power', *Behavioral Science*, no. 2, 1957, pp. 201–5.

4 Jerry F. Hough, *The Struggle for the Third World: Soviet Debates and American Options* (Washington, D.C., Brookings Institution, 1986).

Chapter 2

1 For the text of his report to the Congress, see *Pravda*, 2 February 1956, or *XX s"ezd kommunisticheskoi partii Sovetskogo Soiuza: stenograficheskii otchet*, vol. 1 (Moscow, Gospolizdat, 1956).

2 This was in the form of a telegram from President Voroshilov to Castro. See *Pravda*, 11 January 1959. Before Soviet-Cuban relations were broken during the Cold War period, the Soviet ambassador to the United States acted as envoy to Cuba. The first envoy to Cuba was Maxim Litvinov, who was replaced by Andrei Gromyko when he took over as Soviet ambassador to the USA in August 1943. Gromyko handed in his credentials in Havana on 2 December 1943.

See the interview with Lionel Soto, Cuban ambassador in Moscow up to the summer of 1986, in *Latinskaia Amerika*, no. 5, 1985, pp.75–8.
3 *Noticias de Hoy*, 15 January 1959.
4 *New York Times*, 21 April 1959.
5 *Revolución*, 16 May 1959.
6 *Revolución*, 8 May 1959.
7 *Revolución*, 22 May 1959.
8 See statements of the PSP published in its party organ, *Noticias de Hoy*, on 23 and 26 May 1959.
9 See *Noticias de Hoy*, 26 May 1959, and Blas Roca, 'The Cuban revolution in action', *World Marxist Review*, August 1959, pp. 16–22.
10 Robert Scheer and Maurice Zeitlin, *Cuba: An American Tragedy* (Harmondsworth, Penguin, 1964), p. 98.
11 E.A. Grinevich and B.I. Gvozdarev, *Kuba v mirovoi politike* (Moscow, Mezhdunarodnye otnosheniia, 1984), pp. 98–9. There were rumours that Mikoyan was considering an official trip to Cuba in 1957 and 1958 (i.e., before the revolution), in order to restore diplomatic relations with Batista. In an interview with a Western journalist Mikoyan denied this, stating that 'never have there been such plans, nor are there any now'. See *Les Echos*, 27 June 1958.
12 *Pravda*, 15 February 1960, and Grinevich and Gvozdarev, *Kuba v mirovoi politike*, pp. 98–9.
13 Scheer and Zeitlin, *Cuba: An American Tragedy*, p. 183. See also Nikki Miller and Laurence Whitehead, 'The Soviet Interest in Latin America: An Economic Perspective', in Robert Cassen (ed.), *Soviet Interests in the Third World* (London, Sage for the Royal Institute of International Affairs, 1985), p.117.
14 Scheer and Zeitlin, *Cuba: An American Tragedy*, p. 199.
15 *Pravda*, 9 July 1960.
16 See, for example, *Noticias de Hoy*, 13 July 1960, and *Revolución*, 12 July 1960.
17 *Izvestiia*, 12 July 1960.
18 For Castro's 'I am a Marxist-Leninist, and I shall be a Marxist-Leninist all my life' speech, see *El Mundo*, 3 December 1961, or *Obra Revolucionaria*, 2 December 1961.
19 *Pravda*, 15 April 1962.
20 Strobe Talbott (ed.), *Khrushchev Remembers* (Boston, Little, Brown and Co., 1970), pp. 492–3.
21 Talbott (ed.), *Khrushchev Remembers*, p. 493.
22 Strobe Talbott (ed.), *Khrushchev Remembers: The Last Testament* (Harmondsworth, Penguin, 1974), p. 577.
23 See the interview Castro gave to *Le Monde*, 22 March 1963.
24 Talbott (ed.), *Khrushchev Remembers*, p. 500.

25 Quoted in Carla Anne Robbins, *The Cuban Threat* (Philadelphia, Institute for the Study of Human Issues, 1985), p. 112.
26 *Pravda,* 14 December 1962.
27 *Pravda,* 7 January 1963.

Chapter 3
1 W. Raymond Duncan, *The Soviet Union and Cuba: Interests and Influence* (New York, Praeger, 1985), p. 62.
2 *Bohemia,* 19 March 1965.
3 *Pravda,* 8 August 1965.
4 *Cuba Socialista,* November 1965.
5 Carla Anne Robbins, *The Cuban Threat* (Philadelphia, Institute for the Study of Human Issues, 1985), p. 35.
6 Robbins, *The Cuban Threat,* p. 36.
7 Edward Gonzalez, *Cuba under Castro: The Limits of Charisma* (Boston, Houghton Mifflin Co., 1974), p. 104.
8 *Granma,* 14 March 1967. For a full text of the speech in English, see *Granma Weekly Review,* 19 March 1967.
9 *Granma,* 14 March 1967.
10 *Pravda,* 30 July 1967.
11 The French intellectual, Régis Debray, a close associate of Castro and Guevara, published in 1967 his book *Revolution in the Revolution,* which marked a serious challenge to Soviet orthodox thinking, and hence a challenge to the USSR's leading role in the international revolutionary and communist movement.
12 For these criticisms and a report on the Central Committee meeting, see *Granma Weekly Review,* 11 February 1968.
13 *Granma Weekly Review,* 11 February 1968.
14 *Granma,* 3 January 1968.
15 *Granma Weekly Review,* 11 February 1968.
16 *Pravda,* 30 January 1968. An interesting point here is that, in his speech to the Central Committee, Raúl stated that the Soviet ambassador, Alexandr Alexeev, did not share the views of the microfaction. Alexeev was recalled from Havana in January, and in May Alexandr Soldatov, former Soviet ambassador in London, replaced him as Soviet ambassador to Cuba. See *Granma Weekly Review,* 2 June 1968.
17 See *Granma,* 23 March 1968; Stephen Clissold (ed.), *Soviet Relations with Latin America 1918–68: A Documentary Survey* (Oxford University Press for the Royal Institute of International Affairs, 1970), p. 57; and *The Christian Science Monitor,* 16 July 1969.
18 *Granma Weekly Review,* 19 May 1968.
19 *Granma,* 23 March 1968.

20 Indeed, this was a point made repeatedly to me by officials in Havana while I was on a study visit in the summer of 1986.

21 One should not exaggerate the level of agreement between Castro and Brezhnev at this juncture. For example, at the World Conference of Communist Parties held in Moscow in June 1969 (the final act in the Sino-Soviet debate), the Cubans only sent an 'observer' – and then only after 'exhortations' from Moscow. Carlos Rafael Rodríguez, in his speech at the conference, expressed his opposition to many of the clauses in the final document, and made open criticisms of a number of Soviet foreign policies. He gave only qualified endorsement to Brezhnev's policy of 'peaceful coexistence', and stated, in an obvious criticism of Brezhnev's unfolding 'peace programme', 'Our party cannot adhere to the formulation that states: "The essential orientation of united actions of the anti-imperialist forces continues to be the struggle against the threat of war, for peace in the entire world".' See *Granma Weekly Review*, 15 June 1969.

Chapter 4

1 *Pravda*, 11 July 1969, and *Granma Weekly Review*, 30 November 1969.

2 See *The Times*, 27 July 1970.

3 Carla Anne Robbins, *The Cuban Threat* (Philadelphia, Institute for the Study of Human Issues, 1985), p. 189.

4 *New York Times*, 25 September 1970.

5 Henry Kissinger, *The White House Years* (Boston, Little, Brown and Co., 1979), pp. 632–5.

6 Raymond L. Garthoff, *Detente and Confrontation: American-Soviet Relations from Nixon to Reagan* (Washington, D.C., The Brookings Institution, 1985), p.80.

7 Carlos Rafael Rodríguez, *Letra con Filo*, vol. 2 (Havana, Editorial de Ciencias Sociales, 1983), p. 133.

8 *Granma Weekly Review*, 1 January 1972.

9 *Granma Weekly Review*, 23 July 1972. For information on Cuba's integration into the CMEA, see E.A. Grinevich and B.I. Gvozdarev, *Kuba v mirovoi politike* (Moscow, Mezhdunarodnye otnosheniia, 1984), pp. 152–67.

10 *Vneshniaia Torgovlia*, no. 7, 1984, p.12.

11 See Carmelo Mesa-Lago, *Cuba in the 1970s* (Albuquerque, University of New Mexico Press, 1974), p. 18. However, in assessing Soviet aid to Cuba, we should bear in mind that we are not really dealing with straight US dollars. Much of the Soviet subsidy to Cuba is of course in 'soft currency', so in an important sense it is mistaken to translate this into a dollar equivalence.

12 Isidoro Malmierca, 'Cuban-Soviet relations: a symbol of fraternal friendship', *International Affairs* (Moscow), no. 7, 1985, p. 31.

13 Susan Eckstein, in 'Capitalist constraints on Cuban socialist development', *Comparative Politics*, vol. 12 (1980), no. 3, p. 259, notes that, regarding the establishment of Soviet-type political structures, whilst 'Soviet influence has unquestionably increased . . . internal pressures to institutionalize the revolution undoubtedly account for some of the institutional changes attributed to Soviet dependence'.

14 Valerie Bunce, 'The political economy of the Brezhnev era: the rise and fall of corporatism', *British Journal of Political Science*, vol. 13 (1983), p. 132.

15 See Edward Gonzalez, 'Institutionalization, Political Elites, and Foreign Policies', in Cole Blasier and Carmelo Mesa-Lago (eds), *Cuba in the World* (University of Pittsburgh Press, 1979), pp. 3–36.

16 *Pravda*, 4 July 1973. Kosygin made this point in a speech he gave at a Kremlin dinner in honour of Fidel Castro, who was on an official visit to Moscow.

17 *Soviet News*, 4 February 1974.

18 O. Darusenkov, 'Cuba-USSR: solid friendship', *International Affairs* (Moscow), no. 2, 1974, p. 18.

19 Marc Falcoff, 'Marxist-Leninist Regimes in Central America and the Caribbean', in Uri Ra'anan, Francis Fukuyama, et al., *Third World Marxist-Leninist Regimes: Strengths, Vulnerabilities and US Policy* (Washington, D.C., Pergamon Brassey's, 1985), p. 52.

Chapter 5

1 These figures were given by Fidel Castro in a speech he made in Angola in September 1986. See *Granma Weekly Review*, 21 September 1986.

2 See, for example, *Xinhua News Agency* (Beijing), 22 July 1978.

3 See Keith Somerville, 'Angola: Soviet client state or state of socialist orientation?', *Millennium*, vol. 13 (1984), no. 3, p. 294.

4 This was stressed to me in a personal interview in Havana with a former high-level official in the Cuban Foreign Ministry.

5 See William M. LeoGrande, 'Cuban-Soviet Relations and Cuban Policy in Africa', in Carmelo Mesa-Lago and June S. Belkin (eds), *Cuba in Africa* (University of Pittsburgh Press, 1982), p. 19.

6 Quoted in José Eloy Valdés, 'Notas para un estudio de la situación económica y social de Africa', *Cuba Socialista*, no. 21, 1986, p. 40.

7 See Alexander L. George, 'Detente: The Search for a "Constructive" Relationship', and 'The Basic Principles Agreement of 1972: Origins and Expectations', in Alexander L. George (ed.), *Managing US-Soviet*

Rivalry: Problems of Crisis Prevention (Boulder, CO, Westview, 1983), pp. 17–30, and pp. 107–18. Also see Peter Shearman, *Detente, Soviet-US Relations and the October War in the Middle East, 1973*, Discussion Paper Series no. 5 (Colchester, University of Essex Russian and Soviet Studies Centre, 1985).

8 L.I. Brezhnev, *O vneshnei politike KPSS i sovetskogo gosudarstva: rechi i stati* (Moscow, Izdatel'stvo politicheskoi literatury, 1975), p. 601.

9 For a case study, see Shearman, *Detente, Soviet-US Relations and the October War*.

10 Henry Kissinger, *Years of Upheaval* (Boston, Little, Brown and Co., 1982), pp. 940–5.

11 *Izvestiia*, 21 May 1975.

12 This was made clear to me in a number of interviews with Cuban officials in Havana.

13 Wayne Smith, 'A trap in Angola', *Foreign Policy*, no. 62, Spring 1986, pp. 61–74.

14 LeoGrande, 'Cuban-Soviet Relations', p. 23.

15 Smith, 'A trap in Angola', p. 72.

16 Gabriel García Márquez, 'Operation Carlota', *New Left Review*, no. 101–102, 1977, p. 126.

17 Márquez, 'Operation Carlota', p. 128.

18 *Granma*, 3 January 1976.

19 Michael Taber (ed.), *Cuba's Internationalist Foreign Policy 1975–80: Fidel Castro Speeches* (New York, Pathfinder Press, 1981), p. 92.

20 L.L. Fituni, *Narodnaia Respublika Angola* (Moscow, Nauka, 1985), p. 46. Fituni made this point to me in a personal interview at the African Institute in Moscow, April 1986.

21 Personal interview at IMEMO in Moscow, April 1986.

22 *Granma Weekly Review*, 29 August 1976.

23 See Bruce D. Porter, *The USSR in Third World Conflicts: Soviet Arms and Diplomacy in Local Wars 1945–1980* (Cambridge University Press, 1984), pp. 172–3.

24 Smith, 'A trap in Angola', p. 74.

25 *Pravda*, 30 November 1975. For other reports about US-Chinese collusion, see *Pravda*, 26 October 1975, 5 November 1975, and 19 December 1975.

26 *Pravda*, 2 April 1976.

27 See LeoGrande, 'Cuban-Soviet Relations', who stresses the ideological factor in Cuban foreign policy. In talking to both Soviet and Cuban officials while working on this study, I was struck by the much stronger ideological commitment to 'internationalism' among the Cubans.

28 Márquez, 'Operation Carlota', pp. 134–5.
29 See E.A. Grinevich, 'Chetvert' veka bratskoi druzhby', in S.L. Tikhvinskii (ed.), *Diplomaticheskii vestnik 1985* (Moscow, Mezhdunarodnye otnosheniia, 1986), pp. 75 81.

Chapter 6
1 Christopher Clapham, 'The Soviet Union and the Horn of Africa', paper presented to a workshop on 'The Soviet Union and the Third World', European Consortium for Political Research, Barcelona, March 1985.
2 A.A. Gromyko and B.N. Ponomarev, *Soviet Foreign Policy 1917–1980*, vol. 2 (Moscow, Progress Publishers, 1981), p. 675.
3 Strobe Talbott (ed.), *Khrushchev Remembers: The Last Testament* (Harmondsworth, Penguin, 1974), p. 390.
4 Talbott, *Khrushchev Remembers: The Last Testament*, p. 390.
5 See *Granma Weekly Review*, 9 July 1972.
6 This is cited in Nelson P. Valdes, 'Cuba's Involvement in the Horn of Africa: The Ethiopian-Somali War and the Eritrean Conflict', in Carmelo Mesa-Lago and June S. Belkin (eds), *Cuba in Africa* (University of Pittsburgh Press, 1982), p. 66.
7 Ibid., p. 66.
8 Ibid., p. 67.
9 Bruce D. Porter, *The USSR in Third World Conflicts: Soviet Arms and Diplomacy in Local Wars 1945–1980* (Cambridge University Press, 1984), p. 192.
10 *Pravda*, 16 December 1976, and *Granma*, 16 December 1976.
11 *Granma*, 29 November 1976.
12 *Granma Weekly Review*, 17 April 1976.
13 *Granma*, 26 March 1978. Also in Michael Taber (ed.), *Fidel Castro Speeches* (New York, Pathfinder Press, 1981), pp. 118–19.
14 *Granma Weekly Review*, 17 April 1977.
15 Porter, *The USSR in Third World Conflicts*, p. 196.
16 Valdes, 'Cuba's Involvement in the Horn of Africa', p. 69.
17 *Granma Weekly Review*, 7 August 1977.
18 *Granma Weekly Review*, 7 August 1977.
19 Porter, *The USSR in Third World Conflicts*, p. 203.
20 Porter, *The USSR in Third World Conflicts*, p. 197.
21 Sources for these movements are Porter, *The USSR in Third World Conflicts*, p. 198, *Pravda*, 5 November 1977, and *Pravda*, 7 November 1977.
22 See Porter, *The USSR in Third World Conflicts*, p. 142; Rajan Menon, *Soviet Power and the Third World* (New Haven, CT, Yale University

Press, 1986), p. 142; W. Raymond Duncan, *The Soviet Union and Cuba: Interests and Influence* (New York, Praeger, 1985), p. 134; and Stephen T. Hosmer and Thomas W. Wolfe, *Soviet Policy and Practice Toward Third World Conflicts* (Lexington, MA, Lexington Books, 1983), p.92.

23 Taber (ed.), *Fidel Castro Speeches*, p. 132.
24 *Granma Weekly Review*, 9 April 1978, and Valdes, 'Cuba's Involvement in the Horn of Africa', p. 75.
25 Carla Anne Robbins, *The Cuban Threat* (Philadelphia, Institute for the Study of Human Issues, 1985), p. 230.
26 Taber (ed.), *Fidel Castro Speeches*, p. 122.
27 Valdes, 'Cuba's Involvement in the Horn of Africa', pp. 78–9.
28 See, for example, Valdes, 'Cuba's Involvement in the Horn of Africa'.
29 *Granma*, 15 September 1978.
30 Duncan, *The Soviet Union and Cuba*, p. 135.
31 See, for example, Robbins, *The Cuban Threat*, p. 233.
32 Personal interview, Havana, July 1986.

Chapter 7

1 *Granma Weekly Review*, 22 November 1970, and A.A. Gromyko and B.N. Ponomarev (eds), *Soviet Foreign Policy 1917–1980*, vol. 2 (Moscow, Progress Publishers, 1981), p. 673.
2 See for example B.N. Ponomarev, 'Topical problems in the theory of the revolutionary process', *World Marxist Review*, nos 23–4, 1971; Gabor Kartsag, 'O razvitii revoliutsionnogo protsessa v Latinskoi Amerike', *Latinskaia Amerika*, no 1, 1972, pp. 6–41; and I. Rybalkin, 'Chiliiskii opyt: obshchie zakonomernosti i svoeobrazie revoliutsionnogo protsessa', *Kommunist*, no 8, 1972, pp. 120–7.
3 *Pravda*, 31 March 1971.
4 *Granma Weekly Review*, 19 December 1971.
5 Ibid.
6 Ibid.
7 Ibid.
8 Ibid.
9 *Granma Weekly Review*, 7 October 1973.
10 Jonathan Steele makes this point in his *The Limits of Soviet Power* (Harmondsworth, Penguin, 1984), pp. 218–19.
11 B.N. Ponomarev, 'The world situation and revolutionary process', *World Marxist Review*, no. 6, 1974.
12 S. Mikoyan, *Latinskaia Amerika*, no. 2, 1974.
13 See M.F. Kudachkin, 'Opyt bor'by Kompartii Chili za edinstvo levykh sil i revoliutsionnye preobrazovaniia', *Voprosy Istorii*, no. 5, 1974, pp. 48–60.

14 See B.I. Koval, S.I. Semenov and A.F. Shul'govskii, *Revoliutsonnye protsessy v Latinskoi Amerike* (Moscow, Nauka, 1974). Shul'govskii has a separate chapter on the relationship between 'religion and revolution' (pp. 303–24), in which he argues that 'the strength of the left tendency in Catholicism increases the possibility for an amicable and constructive dialogue and cooperation between communists and believers' (p. 314).

15 See K.N. Brutents, *National Liberation Revolutions Today*, Part II (Moscow, Progress Publishers, 1977), pp. 13–23.

16 Sergei Mikoyan's writings have referred to the NEP as a model for Third World countries undergoing revolutions of national liberation. See S.A. Mikoyan, 'Ob osobennostiakh revoliutsii v Nikaragua i ee urokakh s tochki zreniia teorii i praktiki osvoboditel'nogo dvizheniia', *Latinskaia Amerika*, no. 3, 1980, pp. 34–44.

17 See Mark N. Katz, 'The Soviet-Cuban connection', *International Security*, vol. 8 (1983), no. 1, p. 98.

18 See Sidney Hook's Foreword in Paul Seabury and Walter A. McDougall (eds), *The Grenada Papers* (San Fransisco, Institute for Contemporary Studies, 1984), p. xiv.

19 *New York Times*, 28 October 1983.

20 *Grenada: A Preliminary Report* (Washington, D.C., US Departments of State and Defense, 1983); and Jiri and Virginia Valenta, 'Leninism in Grenada', *Problems of Communism*, July-August 1984, pp. 1–23.

21 *Grenada Documents: An Overview and Selection* (Washington, D.C., US Departments of State and Defense, 1984).

22 *Vneshniaia politika Sovetskogo Soiuza i mezhdunarodnye otnosheniia: sbornik dokumentov* (Moscow, Mezhdunarodnye otnosheniia, 1980).

23 E.A. Grinevich and B.I. Gvozdarev, *Kuba v mirovoi politike* (Moscow, Mezhdunarodnye otnosheniia, 1984), p. 520.

24 *Izvestiia*, 13 September 1979.

25 *Grenada Documents*, no. 26, p. 3.

26 *Grenada Documents*, no. 26, p. 3.

27 *Grenada Documents*, no. 29, p. 2.

28 *Sbornik mezhdunarodnykh dogovorov SSSR* (Moscow, Mezhdunarodnye otnosheniia, 1982), pp. 121–4.

29 Gregory Sandford and Richard Vigilante, *Grenada: The Untold Story* (Lanham, MD, New York and London, Madison Books, 1984), p. 93.

30 *Grenada Documents*, nos 13, 14 and 15.

31 Personal interview in Havana with a former official of the Cuban Foreign Ministry responsible for the Caribbean.

32 Sandford and Vigilante, *Grenada: The Untold Story*, p. 89.

33 *Granma Weekly Review*, 18 January 1981.

34 Sandford and Vigilante, *Grenada: The Untold Story*, p. 89.

35 For elaboration, see Peter Shearman, 'The Soviet Union and Grenada under the New Jewel Movement', *International Affairs*, vol. 61 (1985), no. 4, pp. 661–76.

36 The text of this speech is in Hugh O'Shaughnessy, *Grenada: Revolution, Invasion and Aftermath* (London, Sphere Books, 1984), Appendix 1, pp. 227–42.

37 *Pravda*, 27 October 1983; *Pravda*, 5 November 1983; *Izvestiia*, 3 December 1983; *Pravda*, 4 December 1983; and *Pravda*, 7 December 1983.

38 I. Grigulevich (ed.), *Grenada: History, Revolution, US Intervention* (Moscow, Social Sciences Today, 1984). See p. 9 for the claim regarding the role of the CIA. See also O.T. Darusenkov, *Grenada: mir protiv prestupleniia* (Moscow, Progress Publishers, 1985), and K.A. Khachaturov, *Bol' i gnev Grenady* (Moscow, Sovetskaia Rossiia, 1985),

39 *Grenada Documents*, nos 112 and 113.

40 For this evidence, see Sandford and Vigilante, *Grenada: The Untold Story*, p. 176.

41 Personal interview in Havana with a former Cuban Foreign Ministry official, July 1986.

42 Personal interview in Moscow, April 1986.

43 *International Herald Tribune*, 5 March 1986.

44 Mikoyan, 'Ob osobennostiakh revoliutsii v Nikaragua', p. 36.

45 Ibid., p. 36.

46 I. Grigulevich, *Dorogami Sandino* (Moscow, Molodaia Gvardiia, 1984), p. 4.

47 Grigulevich, *Dorogami Sandino*, p. 5 and p. 14.

48 I.N. Strok, 'Protivoborstvo v Tsentral'noi Amerike: politika SShA i osvoboditel'nyi protsess', *Latinskaia Amerika*, no. 2, 1985, pp. 6 and 14.

49 Strok, 'Protivoborstvo v Tsentral'noi Amerike', p. 6.

50 N.S. Leonov, 'Trevogi i nadezhdy Guatemaly', *Latinskaia Amerika*, no. 7, 1982, p. 51.

51 Grinevich and Gvozdarev, *Kuba v mirovoi politike*, p. 521, and *Izvestiia*, 19 October 1979.

52 *Izvestiia*, 19 October 1979.

53 See Mitchell A. Seligson, 'The Costa Rican Role in the Sandinista Victory', in Thomas W. Walker (ed.), *Nicaragua in Revolution* (New York, Praeger, 1982), pp. 331–43.

54 This quotation is taken from William LeoGrande, 'Cuba and Nicaragua: from the Somozas to the Sandinistas', *Caribbean Review*, vol. 9 (1980), no. 7, pp. 11–14.

55 For texts of the agreements, see Ministerstvo Inostrannykh Del, *Sbornik deistvuiushchikh dogovorov, soglashenii i konventsii, zakluchen-*

nykh SSSR c inostrannymi gosudarstvami, vol. 36 (Moscow, Mezhdunarodnye otnosheniia, 1982), pp. 163–5.

56 In 1982 the volume of Soviet trade with Mexico was 28.8 million roubles, whereas it was 42.5 million roubles with Nicaragua. See Ministerstvo Vneshnei Torgovli, *Vneshniaia torgovlia SSSR v 1983 g.* (Moscow, Finansy i statistiki, 1984), p. 14.

57 Ibid., p. 14.

58 For data on the Sandinista armed forces, see various issues of the *Military Balance*, published annually by the International Institute for Strategic Studies, London.

59 *Granma Weekly Review*, 13 January 1985.

60 Nikki Miller and Laurence Whitehead, 'The Soviet Interest in Latin America', in Robert Cassen (ed.), *Soviet Interests in the Third World* (London, Sage for the Royal Institute of International Affairs, 1985).

61 See Jiri and Virginia Valenta, 'Sandinistas in power', *Problems of Communism*, September-October 1985, pp. 1–28.

62 See V.P. Nikhamin, A.L. Adamashin, et al. (with an introduction by A.A. Gromyko), *Vneshniaia politika Sovetskogo Soiuza*, 3rd edn (Moscow, Politizdat, 1985), p. 70.

63 Ruben Berrios, 'Relations between Nicaragua and the socialist countries', *Journal of Interamerican Studies and World Affairs*, vol. 27 (1985), no. 3, p. 122.

64 Berrios, 'Relations between Nicaragua and the socialist countries'; see table on p. 121.

65 Gerald Segal, 'Sino-Soviet Relations in the Third World', in Cassen (ed.), *Soviet Interests in the Third World*, p. 19. For a detailed examination of Soviet-Vietnamese relations, see Adam Fforde's chapter, 'Economic Aspects of the Soviet-Vietnamese Relationship', in the same Cassen volume, pp. 192–219.

66 *Pravda*, 4 November 1978. The Soviet Union has Treaties of Friendship and Cooperation with the following Third World states: Afghanistan, Angola, Congo, Ethiopia, India, Iraq, Mozambique, Syria, Vietnam, North Yemen, and South Yemen. See Richard F. Staar, *USSR Foreign Policies After Detente* (Stanford, CA, Hoover Institution Press, 1985), p.203.

67 For increasing levels of Soviet aid, see Berrios, 'Relations between Nicaragua and the socialist countries', and Edward Gonzalez, 'The Cuban and Soviet challenge in the Caribbean Basin', *Orbis*, Spring 1985, pp. 73–94.

68 For example, see *Pravda*, 13 March 1986.

69 See *Pravda*, 10 November 1984.

70 This is well argued by Philip D. Stewart, 'Gorbachev and obstacles towards detente', *Political Science Quarterly*, vol. 101 (1986), no. 1, pp. 1–22.

71 Jerry Hough has recently argued that Gorbachev's foreign policy is moving away from a tight bipolar focus on the United States towards a more multipolar focus. See his *The Struggle for the Third World: Soviet Debates and American Options* (Washington, D.C., Brookings Institution, 1986), pp. 283–6.

72 See Andropov's speech to the plenary meeting of the CPSU Central Committee, 15 June 1983, in Yu.V. Andropov, *Speeches and Writings*, 2nd edn (Oxford, Pergamon Press, 1983), pp. 340–59.

73 See *Programma Kommunisticheskoi partii Sovetskogo Soiuza*, novaia redaktsiia (Moscow, Izdatel'stvo politicheskoi literatury, 1986).

74 *Granma Weekly Review*, 24 February 1985.

75 *Granma Weekly Review*, 19 December 1982.

76 *Granma Weekly Review*, 7 October 1984.

77 See Bruce Marcos (ed.), *Nicaragua: The Sandinista People's Revolution. Speeches by Sandinista Leaders* (New York, Pathfinder Press, 1985), p. 182.

Chapter 8

1 See *Fidel Castro: Nothing Can Stop The Course of History* (New York, Pathfinder Press, 1986), p. 28. This 250-page paperback is the text of a wide-ranging interview Castro gave to two Americans (Professor Jeffrey M. Elliot and Congressman Mervyn M. Dymally).

2 *Pravda*, 2 February 1982.

3 V. Volskii, 'Est' Li Vykhod?', *Pravda*, 20 April 1985.

4 Yuri Novopashin, *Problems of Philosophy*, no. 8, 1982.

5 See, for example, Valerie Bunce, *Do New Leaders Make a Difference?* (Princeton University Press, 1981), and George W. Breslauer, *Khrushchev and Brezhnev as Leaders: Building Authority in Soviet Politics* (London, George Allen and Unwin, 1982).

6 *Soviet News*, 12 February 1986.

7 *Granma Weekly Review*, 14 December 1986.

8 *Izvestiia*, 16 May 1985.

9 *Granma Weekly Review*, 11 August 1985.

10 *Granma Weekly Review*, 21 July 1985.

11 *Granma Weekly Review*, 4 December 1986.

12 *Latin America Weekly Report*, 11 December 1986.

Related titles

The Nuclear Predicament: Explorations in Soviet Ideology
Stephen Shenfield

Ideological debate is one component of the intellectual background to Soviet policy-making. This paper explores how Soviet writers wrestle with the challenge to their ideology that is posed by the threat of nuclear war. What, for example, is the relationship between the values of peace and of socialism? What drives the arms race? Is capitalism inherently militaristic, or is a demilitarized capitalism conceivable? Is the outcome of history predetermined or open? It is shown that the range of permissible views is wider than often assumed, and that the constraints of Soviet ideology do not exclude evolution towards a more cooperative approach to international security.

Western Economic Statecraft in East-West Relations
Philip Hanson

This Chatham House Paper is an assessment of those East-West trade policies of Western governments that are intended to serve the purposes of foreign policy, or which have important foreign-policy implications. The assessment is mainly of policies directed at the USSR and its allies. The starting-point is the question, what are the most appropriate policies for the Western alliance as a whole? The author distinguishes three domains of East-West trade policy, each with its own rationale and instruments: sanctions or leverage, designed to alter particular Soviet-bloc policies; the strategic embargo, whose purpose is (or should be) the protection of Western security through hindering Warsaw Pact access to militarily useful technology in which the West has a lead; and long-term strategy in East-West relations, in which there is a choice between economic warfare and detente.

The Soviet Union and India
Peter J. S. Duncan

India is the only non-communist country in the Third World with which the Soviet Union has managed to maintain friendly relations over a prolonged period. To what extent is the closeness of India to the USSR on many foreign-policy issues the result of a coincidence of interests rather than Soviet influence? This paper assesses the balance of costs and benefits to the USSR of its considerable economic and military involvement with India, and concludes by examining the implications of possible shifts in Soviet policy in the region for Western links with India.

Routledge & Kegan Paul

9790